The Italian Theatre Today

The Italian Theatre Today:
Twelve Interviews

by
Alba Amoia

❧

The Whitston Publishing Company
Troy, New York
1977

To C. P.

The following study was made possible by a grant from the City University of New York Faculty Research Program.

TABLE OF CONTENTS

PREFACE

Very little is known about the Italian theatre today, unfortunately. Italian critics, most of whom are playwrights, praise only their predecessors -- long dead. They have stopped at Pirandello. Some, exceptionally, acknowledge Ugo Betti too. It is sad, but in Italy there is a long established tradition never to praise the living dramatists. Consequently, critics are no longer asked about the new Theatre. We are all too familiar with their answers about the old. Who can tell us about the new Theatre, then? The playwrights? Would they be objective? Can they? I can say that in my life I have never heard an Italian playwright praise a colleague. Never! (In America, Tennessee Williams is known to have encouraged and promoted many new dramatists.)

Alba Amoia had the brilliant idea of interviewing Italian actors, hoping finally to discover the mystery of Italian dramaturgy today. Her experience was unique and always illuminating. Her questions are clever and very revealing. The answers are often amazing. Some are masterpieces of elusiveness -- "Italian style." They demonstrate very clearly why no one knows much about the new Italian playwrights. Few mention them. There is never any enthusiasm for their work. Obviously the "establishment" does not want this well-kept secret let out of the bag.

Some statements in the interviews are, nevertheless, honest and basic. Paolo Grassi says: "Whereas so many countries are proud of their culture, Italy lives its culture but doesn't exalt it. If there is one country...where priority of the national product does not exist-- it's Italy." I agree completely. Giorgio Albertazzi says: "You're very naive to think that in Italy it is possible to set up a committee of experts which will make objective judgments." This is absolutely true. Such a thing is impossible. The Italians *cannot* be objective. Political passion distorts their views. A right-wing critic will never praise a political play. A left-wing critic will never praise a non-polemic play. Since the Italian theatre is predominantly liberal and progressive, the big newspapers, and radio and television (controlled by the Government), will ignore or condemn anything too theatrical or too progressive. As a result, even an excellent play dies after an average of thirty performances.

Alba Amoia was very keen in catching her interviewees off guard. She elicited illuminating reactions. She asks Franco Fano about the panorama of the Italian theatre today. He cannot come up with one writer! Not even one! She asks him about a "revival of the Italian theatre in the early seventies." He mentions only last season's productions. Mario Missiroli's... *Inspector General;* Luigi Squarzina's... *Mother Courage*... The playwrights are dead; long live the directors!

In the interview with director Franco Enriquez, Alba Amoia gets some more interesting admissions. "Which contemporary dramatists do you consider most highly? " — "Beckett, Stoppard, Pinter." She asks Turi Ferro, the actor-director, if there is a revival of the Italian theatre in sight. The answer is: "...there are few people who write for the theatre." (Five hundred new plays are written every year in Italy; are they read?) She asks Arnoldo Foà why Italians prefer foreign dramatists. The answer is interesting: "Because we are a people who generally denigrate ourselves." True! She tries to ask Luigi De Filippo about his great uncle Eduardo De Filippo, one of the best Italian playwrights today. The answers are often evasive. He says, obliquely: "Eduardo doesn't renew his repertory. He only performs his own plays." It is interesting also to note that the actors Albertazzi, Foà, and Luigi De Filippo talk a lot about the few plays they have written, and very little about other plays they are supposed to read and know.

Alba Amoia keeps asking questions. She wants to know. We all want to know. The scene seems bleak. Is it possible that a country that can produce great novelists, poets and film-makers cannot produce playwrights? I receive and read at least one hundred new plays a year from Italy. Some of them are first-rate. For the record, I want to mention the names of several playwrights who have been active since World War II, in the new, democratic Italy. Some of the best are: Alfredo Balducci, Enrico Bassano, Massimo Binazzi, Franco Brusati, Luigi Candoni, Salvato Cappelli, Luciano Codignola, Eduardo De Filippo, Vincenzo Di Mattia, Diego Fabbri, Dario Fo, Dacia Maraini, Renato Mainardi, Robert Mazzucco, Mario Moretti, Aldo Nicolaj, Giuliano Parenti, A. Gaetano Parodi, G. P. Griffi, C. M. Pensa, Leonardo Sciascia, Luigi Squarzina, Carlo Terron, Massimo Dursi, and... at least twenty more. An Italian theatre does exist, and

Alba Amoia is helping us discover it.

Mario Fratti[1]
New York, May 1974

---

[1] Mario Fratti is an Italian playwright now living in New York City. His plays, *The Cage, The Suicide, The Academy, The Return, The Bridge, Mafia, Che Guevara, Eleonora Duse, The Refusal, The Brothel, The Family, The Gift, The Wish, The Refrigerators, The Chinese Friend, The Roman Guest, Races, The Victim,* and *Chile 1973* have been produced in over three hundred theatres in fourteen languages. They have been published by Dell, Colliers, Macmillan, Enact, Breakthough, Proscenium, Edgemoor, Crown, McGraw-Hill, and Prentice-Hall.

INTRODUCTION

The observer of the contemporary Italian scene is struck by the number of crises that face the nation: political, economic, educational, religious, linguistic, sociological and ecological. To the list must be added periods of "theatrical malaise," perhaps not of crisis proportion, but indicative of a continuing search for a unified theatre in a nation of twenty highly differentiated regions. Two decades of Fascist censorship had their effect on Italian theatrical style as well as on the national character, which is difficult to define and is not reflected in a specifically Italian "national theatre." Although homogeneous in many respects and possessed of a cultural, traditional and linguistic unity, especially on the elitist level, Italian society is nevertheless quite diversified. Historically, Italy lacks what France, for example, had in order to create a national theatre: independence, political unity, and a central government with a capital city. As Paolo Grassi points out in his interview below, it is difficult to find the true "center" of Italy. Rome may be the governmental capital, but Milan, as the seat of the anti-Fascist Resistance, is considered the "moral capital" of the country. Milan is the city that attracted the intellectuals among the generation that grew up under the dictatorship; the city that was sensitive to cultural problems; and the first city to establish a Stabile (Permanent) Theatre — the *Piccolo Teatro di Milano* — inaugurated on May 14, 1947.

The state-subsidized Stabile Theatres that exist in Italy in addition to private groups are defined as "necessary instruments for the diffusion of drama as a public service, through a repertory inspired by artistic standards." The Stabile Theatres aim for a continuity of presentations, a solidity of theatrical structure (so that the concept holds up even as a business enterprise), and a theatrical policy that reconciles esthetic demands with new social concerns. After Milan, Rome, Genoa and Turin set up Stabile Theatres, and in the 1960's solidity was achieved in parts of the country. The Stabile of Genoa, for example, under the directorship of Ivo Chiesa, who was later joined by Luigi Squarzina, attracted an extraordinarily large public in a city traditionally hostile to theatre. For fourteen seasons, Genoa's Stabile brought sixty-eight productions to sixty-two Italian cities and twenty-four foreign cities. Bologna, Florence, Venice, Bolzano and Trieste tried to organize theatrical groups, but subsequently had to abandon efforts in the face of insufficient public support and local cooperation. In the South the De Filippos, after intitial hopes had been aroused, had to relinquish the reconstructed San Ferdinando and the restored Mercadante theatres in Naples. Bari's theatrical efforts were feeble, to say the least. Theatre in Sardegna remained practically non-existent, but Sicily succeeded in establishing two Stabile Theatres, one in Palermo and one in Catania. Rome's Stabile closed down, however, and the first proponents of the need for a national theatre seated in the capital lacked cement for its structural foundation. Thus, the proposed network of Stabile Theatres throughout the regions of Italy, which would eventually link up all the major cities, never materialized.

****

Culturally, Italy is handicapped by the fact that basically it is not one country. It is twenty countries, and affinities can nowhere be found between a Venetian and a Sicilian, for example. The former loves Goldoni; the latter does not understand him, not only because of a language difference, but because Goldoni represents a different world with different sentiments. More affinities can be found between a Florentine and a Britisher, as Giorgio Albertazzi will point out below. The twenty Italian regions have little in common with each other; there are vast differences between the industrialized North and the underdeveloped South, and, as the following interviews will show, there is no one theatre that suits all Italians. There has been no tradition of an Italian repertory that reflects dramatic literature on the national level.

It is significant that while in the decades following the Renaissance, England had Shakespeare and the Elizabethans, France had Corneille, Racine and Molière, and Spain had Calderon de la Barca and Lope de Vega, the most significant theatrical expression in Italy was the *commedia dell'arte*. One of the explanations for this difference lies in the fact that Italy has not had the opportunity to approach moral, religious, and political problems in a *social* way, and thus the theatre has not been able to be a faithful "mirror of society." The need for an expressive integration of poet and society has never been filled. At the end of the nineteenth century, only Machiavelli and Goldoni were considered historically and artistically meaningful dramatic authors. Today, modern stagings of Goldoni by Giorgio Strehler and Luchino Visconti have been efforts to deepen the historic and artistic dialogue between the Venetian playwright and the contemporary public. Young actors today frequently revive Machiavelli's *The Mandrake (La Mandragola)* because they see in it a truth that complements "official truth," and their staging of such a play becomes a political act.

Even these noteworthy efforts, however, have not permitted the theatre, which is a form of social and collective art, to find its true place in Italian society. Drama needs the coordinated and simultaneous involvement of author and actor, impresario and scenographer, mechanic and stagehand. As Gaston Baty has indicated, dramatic art is great only when poet, actors and spectators are all participants in the ritual. Splintered Italy does not possess the basis for such a relationship. Theatre, as a dialogue, has an interlocutory immediacy based on a common feeling. It is, therefore, a more democratic form of art than Italy is yet able to experience.

Certainly a "repertory inspired by artistic standards" is not missing from Italy's theatres (the most important of which in the early 1970's seem to be the newly established Theatre of Rome, and the Stabiles of Milan, Catania, L'Aquila, Turin, Genoa and Trieste), but the predominant authors in the repertories are Pirandello, Shakespeare, Brecht, Goldoni and Chekhov, who scarcely constitute a modern *national* repertory. Even if we include an updated Giovanni Verga[1], Italo Svevo, Vitaliano Brancati, Ugo Betti and Diego Fabbri, we still do not have enough "cement" for a national repertory theatre. Fabbri is, perhaps, the most "involved," but he is orthodox and European rather than Italian, like Ugo Betti before him. Pirandello, who was far ahead of his time, remains the principal dramatic communicator of sentiments proper to Italian society, and finds his most significant interpretation today rather than at the time he wrote. Courageous, enlightened witnesses and commentators, responsible for a complete and moral judgment of society, are lacking today, despite sporadic exceptions, nor has any author answered satisfactorily the questions asked by contemporary Italian youth. The few Italian playwrights whose names do appear in the repertories are eclipsed by foreign moderns: Brecht, Ionesco, Beckett, Miller, Williams, Osborne, Wesker, Pinter, etc. There is a difficult theatre-public relationship in Italy that complicates the issue: for reasons of commercialism, or prestige, or current style, theatres are forced to stage "sure" authors, so the Italian spectator lacks sufficient opportunity for direct contact with contemporary playwrights. Furthermore, even today, the Italian theatre continues to exploit a public predisposition for *divertissement,* which prevents the development of a national dramatic tendency. A new model of theatrical organization has emerged in Italy's industrial-socio-economic triangle of development, where theatre has proceeded to become a consumer item, subject to the same manipulation as other commercial products. (Cf. Franco Enriquez' interview, below.)

Italians will applaud Ionesco because it is fashionable to do so, but we can sense their mental reservations inasmuch as they have lost their sense of humor with respect to life's daily situations. Italy has never had a Brecht, nor can one be improvised, but Italians are seeking a theatre that will force them to think. For them, Brecht is a man of faith, and one of the most complete, revolutionary men of the theatre whose honesty of intention and action is undeniable. His theatre is epic rather than bourgeois, and in Italy the traditional bourgeois spectator is fast disappearing. The new spectator no longer seeks "illusion"; he wants a rational and disenchanted relationship with the stage and expects the theatre to concern itself with such important problems as the conflict between the bourgeois and the socialist worlds. The dramatic form best suited to treat this theme would be satire, which recaptures the spirit of ancient Rome and of the *commedia dell'arte* and is, therefore, congenial to the Italian nature. Satire, however, is absent from contemporary Italian dramaturgy because of a basic political conservatism and self-imposed censorship by Italy's writers. (Cf. interview with Paolo Grassi, below.)

Also lacking in Italy is a new theatrical language that would repudiate both realistic dialects (which on stage become a caricature of reality) and the academic language, official Italian (which is a foreign language to most Italians). What is needed is the invention of a new language that both assimilates the spirit and the philosophy of dialects, and takes into account a free people that expresses itself synthetically and nervously, without banal or useless words.

If the old structures are unsuited to the new perspectives, then the panorama of theatrical groups in Italy — from old travelling companies to the Stabile Theatres — will have to show more of an ability to solve today's problems. The recent phenomenon of the "great directors" — Strehler, Gassman, Visconti — who respond to public exigencies, is a venture in this direction. Lavishing care and money, they are trying to attract a popular mass to the theatre and create a climate of interest among the Italian public as a whole. There is still, however, a feeling of uncertainty about the stability and fortune of the future of dramatic art in Italy. Between 1950 and 1959, eight million spectators were lost to the Italian theatre, and those who remained went to see a star or a sensational play. During those years, attempts were made to strengthen theatrical culture by bringing the schools to the theatre, thereby creating a new public among the young. Proposals were made to produce plays by Schools of Dramatic Art and to take them on tour in the provinces, keeping the price of tickets under five hundred lire (about eighty-five cents), and getting students to subscribe. Efforts continue along these lines today, especially by the Theatre of Rome, but it is still too early to evaluate their results.

The malaise in the contemporary Italian theatre has two aspects. The first is historic: a lack of a true, dramatic tradition in poetry that dates from the Renaissance, an era that favored literary and academic theatre closed to the masses and created a vacuum that has never been filled. The second is a socio-economic structural weakness of more recent vintage: movies and television as forms of popular art, an evolution in the Italian way of thinking and living, and the transformation of the theatrical spectacle into a commercial "product" costing much and in little demand — all have contributed to the siphoning off of an eligible public. Although the tide seems to be turning in the early 1970's, the problem remains whether the theatre in Italy today can arouse a basically skeptical public to a point that will enable a meaningful national repertory to be created. The present period lies somewhere between the conservative arriere-gardism of the war and immediate post-war years, and the iconoclastic avant-gardism which, personified by Carmelo Bene, is germinating "off-Rome," "off-Florence" — i.e. in the small, "underground" theatres of the cities. As things stand now, however, if the State did not intervene with subsidies, dramatic art probably would not exist in Italy today — at least not in its traditionally organized form.

The interviews that follow were conducted in an attempt to elicit from twelve men connected with the Italian theatre their views on theatrical nationalism and the divergencies among Italy's theatre-going public. Although none of the twelve admits that "theatre is dead" in Italy, responses range from the deeply pessimistic to the highly optimistic, which demonstrates the Italian capacity to see one thing several ways, in true Pirandellian spirit.

For the publication of these interviews, my thanks are due to Professor Stephen Goode, Professor Bettina Knapp, and Mr. Emidio Celani.

Alba Amoia

---

[1] Cf. Franco Zeffirelli's 1965 version of *The She-Wolf (La Lupa)* with Anna Magnani, and Diego Fabbri's version of Verga's *Mastro Don Gesualdo,* produced by the Stabile of Catania in 1973, with Turi Ferro.

PAOLO GRASSI

Interviewer's Note:

Paolo Grassi is a theatrical director, drama critic, and the founder-director of the first Stabile Theatre in Italy *(Piccolo Teatro di Milano)*; recently he became manager of Milan's la Scala Opera. Born on October 30, 1919, Grassi began his theatrical experiences in 1937; four years later he founded the avant-garde *Palcoscenico (Stage),* an experimental group including Giorgio Strehler, with whom he maintained a close collaboration at the *Piccolo Teatro.* He worked as drama critic for the Milanese newspaper, *Avanti!* from 1945 to 1947, while contributing to several theatrical publications as well. He returned to directing in 1946, founded the *Piccolo* in 1947, and in 1956 organized the Venice Theatre Company, which toured abroad with Diego Fabbri's *Between Two Crosses (Processo a Gesù)* during the 1955-56 season.

Grassi is Italy's main post-war advocate of a radical renewal of the Italian theatre. He believes that municipal theatres must be created, to which all classes and especially the masses will be attracted, and whose repertories should be modelled on those of the most advanced European theatres. The repertories chosen by Grassi — which have been brought throughout Europe and to South America — maintain the highest cultural level and include Shakespeare, Molière, Goldoni, Gozzi, Ibsen, Becque, Chekhov, Sartre, Brecht, Pirandello and Fabbri.

Q.   Do you think it is possible to create a national Italian theatre comparable to the Comédie Française?

A.   The Comédie Française was created in the seventeenth century, in a country of great theatrical tradition and activity. Today, the Comédie Française is a museum. I don't know whether there is this urgent need today to create a national theatre for Italy. In London, it's conceivable, inasmuch as London is the political, cultural, moral and intellectual capital of Great Britain; in France, it's understandable because Paris has always been the center of France; but in Italy, where would you put the center? Besides Rome, the capital, there is a culturally, morally, economically, politically strong city: Milan. Milan would have to become a colony of the national theatre which is active in Rome; whereas the Italian theatre has had, and has now, in Milan, its strongest points of reference. I don't know. I would say it's a false problem, a false aim, a way of inventing a problem that would become a big government project involving authors and directors. It would become a pluralistic theatre, i.e., the negation of a theatre. A theatre should not be a museum, available to any director or to any artistic contribution. A real theatre— a theatre that goes beyond history— is one that reflects the times. What is the Burgtheater in Vienna? The Comédie Française in German. But has the history of the theatre in Europe passed through the Comédie Française and the Burgtheater or rather through Piscator's Volksbühne, through Jacques Copeau's reforms, through the cartel of Jouvet, Pitoëff, Baty, Dullin, through the TNP — not any TNP, but that of Jean Vilar, through Planchon at Villeurbanne, through Strehler in Milan? The Soviet theatre is famous throughout the world for the contributions, before and during the great years of the Revolution, of Meyerhold, Tairoff, Stanislavsky and Danchenko — but not because there was a big national theatre to which each one made his contribution. A big, national theatre that is undefined becomes a big and unqualified supermarket.

Q.   From the sociological point of view, does the Italian theatre exist for a particular class?

A.   In the nineteenth century, the Italian theatre was a theatre for the bourgeoisie, a class that knew exactly what it wanted and constructed the theatre, as it were, for its own use and consumption; and that determined, economically, artistically, and culturally, with some negative but many positive results, the life of dramatic and lyric theatre. Today, the bourgeoisie in Italy does

not have the weight it had in the nineteenth century.
We are not in a state of proletariat govenment, but certainly we are in a stage of transformation of society; we
are going through a stage of disappearance of the aristo-
cracy, diminished bourgeois power, and greater proletariat power — to the point of making a difference in Italian
life. Today, for a theatre to be alive and useful, and necessary to the national community, it cannot be a class
theatre, but a theatre open to all citizens of all classes.

Q.   Italian repertories include many foreign authors (Shakespeare, Ibsen, Feydeau, Brecht, Miller, Beckett, etc.) but
relatively few contemporary Italian authors.   Why?

A.   Italy is a 2,000-year old society, as contrasted with America, a young country, and England, which is four centur-
ies old. Italy has a long background of civilization. We
had a theatre 2,000 years ago, with Plautus and Terence.
It was a great theatre, and a great civilization. Old countries, with ancient civilizations, do not have the nationalistic urges that young countries have.   Italy is not a
nationalistic country — absolutely not. Not on the political and military, and even less on the cultural level.
Whereas so many countries are proud of their culture,
Italy lives its culture but doesn't exalt it. If there is one
country that has wide open curiosity about foreign cul-
tures, if there is one country where priority of the national product does not exist — it's Italy. If we had a
large contemporary repertory, we would present it. But
which country in the whole world has one today? Germany had a great theatre for twenty years, and yet did
not present its contemporary authors. Today, they give
Peter Weiss and some others. There is some upsurge of
contemporaries, but you certainly can't say that the
German repertory is based on contemporary German
authors. England had its great moment with the Angry
Young Men for ten or eleven years, but you can't say that
the promises of Pinter, Wesker and other authors have
been kept. Today England may have five great authors,
but neither the U.S.A. nor the U.S.S.R. has that many.
The U.S. had a good theatre before Broadway devoured
its outstanding writers, before Clifford Odets went to
sell himself to Hollywood. So it's not a situation peculiar

to Italy.   France, which used to have a great national
repertory theatre, no longer has it today.   I am convinced that more could be done in Italy today to help the
contemporary Italian repertory.   I am convinced that
more could be presented if only there were a little more
good will, more faith, more work devoted to creating an
Italian dramaturgy.

Q.   Those few Italian authors that write today — have they a
particular message to communicate to the public?

A.   Every author has his message, his style, and his own
things to communicate to society. At this moment, there
is an Italian writer, Massimo Dursi, whose *Bluebeard (Il
Barba blù)* is being presented at the Piccolo Teatro of
Milan; his *The Outbreak of the Woolcombers (Il Tumulto
dei Ciompi)* is being given by an excellent company
touring Italy; and his *The Passer-by (Il Passatore)*[1] is at
the Stabile Theatre of Bolzano. For many years, he was
not presented at all, and this year three theatres are giving
his plays. So if we are to judge at this moment the favor
being showered on Dursi, it is extraordinary.

Q.   Why is there no politico—satirical theatre in Italy, which
seems to offer a vast field for it?

A.   There is *political* theatre, but the political *cabaret* does
not exist, nor does political *satire* on stage. First of all,
we are a nation that lives in the same house as the Vatican. We have two governments in Italy: the government
of the Republic and the Vatican (something that everyone must consider, including Americans, and especially
Catholic Americans; it's much easier to be a Catholic in
Munich or in Paris than in Rome, or Milan, or New
York). Secondly, Italy is the country of the Counter-
Reformation, i.e. of Catholic conservatism.   Whereas
Luther effected his great Protestant Reformation, we effected the Counter-Reformation. We are the country in
which the Roman Apostolic Church has killed Galileo's
political and scientific freedom, and burned at the stake
Giordano Bruno and Thomas Campanella. The seven-
teenth century in Italy — a century of thinkers and philosophers— the Italy of science, of philosophy, of re-

search, found its roads closed by the Catholic Church. Thirdly, we have not had a French Revolution — whether for good or for ill— which is a European and particularly French patrimony. Fourthly, we have a young state — one hundred years old — and an authoritarian state. Whereas in Greece, 2,500 years ago, Aristophanes or a Greek poet could ridicule their leaders on the stage, with the most biting satire, we cannot ridicule the President of the Republic or a well-known political figure. Television doesn't do it either; there is a political predisposition. Now General de Gaulle was a dictator — not a Nazi dictator, but a dictator, an autocrat. In France, despite Gaullism and de Gaulle, there was always a certain liberty. *Le Canard enchaîné* mocked him in its ferocious cartoons, and Henri Tissot mimicked the General in all the bistros in Paris. Just imagine anyone in Italy mimicking the President of the Republic — a Saragat, a Leone, a Fanfani. It's just unthinkable! So writers impose on themselves a self-censorship, and political satire just doesn't exist. In Germany, it was easy. There was all the great political satire of 1919-1920. And even in Italy, from 1910 to 1925, before Fascism, there was a lot of rich political satire, which no longer exists today. Fascism stopped it, first of all, and then it was also stopped by another form of Fascism, which is respect for institutions. It is a hypocritical imposition. In any case, we cannot speak ill of priests, cardinals, carabinieri, nor the armed forces. A text such as *Oh What A Lovely War!* by Joan Littlewood, in Italy, in the original Anglo-Saxon version, cannot be produced. We had to present it in a watered-down form. We cannot attack our army, we can't speak ill of the air force; everything is heroic; everything is untouchable. So, on the level of a political rally, or in a political newspaper, you can get away with it, but in a political cabaret, or in the theatre, which obeys so many laws, you won't find political satire.

Q.   How do Italians react to avant-garde theatre? to Ionesco? to the theatre of cruelty? the theatre of the absurd? to Beckett, to Arrabal, etc.?

A.   Well, very well. These authors are well-known and are

often presented in Italy. Ionesco triumphed with his
Rhinoceros; today he is considered a classic. The so-
called avant-garde theatre, or the theatre of the absurd,
or of cruelty, or what has been salvaged of Antonin
Artaud, artificial or not, have all been punctually recognized even here in Italy. The theatre of gestures, the
theatre of imagery, the theatre of vision.... Today, we
are in the theatre of imagery. From this point of view,
I am a dissident. I am opposed to all these types of
dramaturgy and theatricality. I have always maintained,
together with Strehler, together with Planchon, with the
Berliner Ensemble, with Vilar, that in the years 1970-
1980, we should be creating and practicing, after the
slaughter of World War II, a theatre for man, for man's
reason, and not an irrational theatre. Now, the creation
of men in decomposition, in garbage cans, by a great
writer, Samuel Beckett, corresponds to a vision of a
crumbling world that does not belong to us. The rituals
and solipsisms of Grotowski, who confines eighty spectators in a room for a certain rendition of Calderón de la
Barca — I reject them. I am opposed to the theatre of
gestures, the Open Theatre, all the anarchistic mystification of the Living Theatre (which derived from Pirandello
and Brecht, and from the jungle-city, but ended up by
being the most uncontrolled ideological anarchy in the
name of liberty — abstract liberty does not exist, you
know). Personally, I am violently against these flower
children, these phenomena that are a flight from reality.
This type of theatre champions Ionesco's mystification,
or irrationality, or the gesticulative. I believe that society
should work for man, for man's betterment; that the
theatre of words, the theatre of reason — Brecht's dramaturgy and esthetic — should be the theatre of our time
and of our century. But for this we would need a rational youth. Instead, we have youth that for the most part
takes drugs, dresses in blue jeans, and travels in beard
and long hair. It's a return to Romanticism. At the same
time, man is exploring space and landing on the moon.
So there is a contradiction. Perhaps it's not such an easy
problem. Perhaps the world today does not offer those
ideal concepts through which youth can recognize itself
in society. So youth seeks its physiognomy and seeks its
place in forms, manifestations and gestures *against* this

society. However, it's sad to think that so many years after Schiller, we have returned to that form of Romanticism. That's my personal opinion. I know it is not shared by many and that it is unpopular in Italy. I do not believe in the theatre of imagery, because we have the movies for imagery; I don't believe in the theatre of gestures, because the gesticulative is for animals and not men. Men must gesture, but gesture is a function of words. What distinguishes us from fish and animals is the *word*. If we don't use words, we reduce the theatre to an aquarium for lobsters that move about splendidly. But what distinguishes man is the *word* and *reason*.

Q.   Would you say, then, that your philosophy of the theatre is one of rationality, esthetics, and pragmatism?

A.   Exactly.

Q.   Are there differences in theatrical tastes between Northern and Southern Italians?

A.   There are differences in frequency of attendance. Torino has much more theatre than Messina, Bologna much more than Taranto. So obviously it's not so much a difference of tastes but rather of frequenting the theatre, of preparation, culture, and knowledge. The South, even in its theatrical culture, suffers from its state of economic inferiority compared to the North. So it has fewer theatres and less opportunity, and therefore less theatrical culture. But the imagination and the intelligence of Southerners merit as much theatre as the North.

Q.   But the repertories of the North and South would differ, wouldn't they?

A.   Basically, I think so. I would say that the South (with some exceptions) is less sensitive to changes in style, less sensitive to taste values and to certain cosmopolitan values of theatrical taste. I think the South seeks a more direct theatrical experience and not these international innovations and these new theatrical phenomena that are so much in style today.

Q.   Will you explain the concept in Italy of the "theatre in the schools"?

A.   Even though results have varied, according to the city in which the experiment is carried out, we have always considered dramatization a formative component of each individual. There are various levels of theatre in the schools: children's theatre (i.e. created by children— the dramatic game played by children); theatre *for* children; theatre *for* young people; cultural theatre for adults; and university theatre, presented *for* the students and *by* the students. As a method of civic and cultural self-education, as a didactic instrument of civic and cultural formation of the individual, the theatre is still irreplaceable. From this point of view, we support all theatrical activity — even in schools, from the lowest level to the university.

Q.   What are the financial problems facing the Italian theatre today?

A.   There are no state funds for the theatre; it is funded through yearly assignments made to the Ministry for the Performing Arts. The entire Italian theatre is aided by the government, whether it be the public theatre (i.e. the big Stabile theatres), or the coöperative company created by an actor, or a manager's company which has private capital. Behind every curtain that goes up, there is always government aid, which can be small, large, very small, very large, but there is no curtain that goes up before which, behind which, and after which there is no state aid. In my opinion, this should be so; the artistic decadence of the American theatre, for example, is due to the fact that Broadway is engaged in business; and business is the negation of art; from which results the flight from Broadway. The phenomenon of off-Broadway is the phenomenon of a flight by theatrical people away from a place that was a place of art but now has become a business center. Business in the theatre, one time out of a thousand, is art; nine hundred and ninety-nine times it's business and has no relationship to art. I think that in the entire civilized world, only the United States and Great Britain do not have a national policy for the theatre. France has one; Italy has one; even

Spain has one.   Germany, Austria and Switzerland all
have one.   All of Europe spends for the theatre—not to
keep it alive but so that the theatre, in economic freedom, can remain a fact of art and culture.   And the two
big countries with free economies — the United States
and Great Britain—up to now have only made some gestures but have not really formulated a policy for their
theatres.

Q.   What do you see in the future for the Italian theatre?

A.   I would say that the *present* is good. I would say that the
first goal for the future should be the *diffusion* of the
theatre — quantitatively — over the entire area of the Republic.   There are entire regions, especially in the South,
that have very little theatre.   And justice demands that
the entire Republic have theatre.   So, an increase in
quantity; and a defense and an increase of quality; and
an increase of those structures that guarantee, in time,
the continuity of the quality and the quantity of the
Italian theatre.   With regard to the stage, one can say
that Italy is and always has been a country of theatrical
producers, scenographers, costume designers, etc., so
there are no particular problems except those of one or
two well-known personalities. Our stage has always maintained a level of quality, and, as far as our dramaturgy is
concerned, I have already said that more should be done
to engage a greater number of contemporary dramatists
in the theatrical and cultural life of society in Italy today.

---

[1] Published in the U.S.A. in *Drama & Theatre,* State University
College, Fredonia, N.Y. (Henry F. Salerno, Ed.)

FRANCO ENRIQUEZ

Interviewer's Note:

Franco Enriquez, the Director of the Theatre of Rome, is a theatrical and television director, born in Florence on November 20, 1927. Early in his career, he assisted Luchino Visconti and Giorgio Strehler, and made his debut as director with George Bernard Shaw's *Caesar and Cleopatra* in 1951. Enriquez has directed opera since 1953, his latest achievement being the production of Verdi's *Simon Boccanegra* at the Arena of Verona in 1973.

Long known for the versatility and vigor he brought to the performances of his popular Company of Four (Enriquez, Valeria Moriconi, Glauco Mauri, and Emanuele Luzzati), Franco Enriquez' thirst for experimentation in the theatre is also becoming legendary.

Q.   You were named Director of the new Theatre of Rome[1] in August 1972. Will you tell us about your first season, 1972-73?

A.   It was a rich and eventful season, and for the first time a city like Rome— a capital like Rome—felt the presence of theatre conceived as a public service in the same way that other Italian cities, like Milan, Genoa and Turin, had succeeded in recent years in setting up theatres dedicated to the service of the public. Rome, for an infinite number of reasons, too numerous to recall here, had never succeeded in all these years in establishing a functional structure and a dialectic instrument for theatrical dissemination in keeping with its rank as capital of our country. This is really the first year in which Rome has a municipal theatre. Although we have gone through thick and thin and have made errors, our pilot efforts were rewarded with much better results than expected.

We have now laid down lines of operation, and there is no going back: we must develop further. When I was appointed Director of the Theatre of Rome in 1972 (known then as the Stabile Theatre of Rome), my first concern was to launch a series of theatrical initiatives that would be polyvalent and multidirectional. I was basically concerned with using the Argentina Theatre as the central showplace for Rome's theatrical activity, but at the same time going beyond the confines of the Argentina and branching out into the areas surrounding Rome — that is, the theatrical decentralization of this megalopolis. We sought to be in touch with and provide incentives for theatrical activity in the entire region of Lazio and in certain geographic centers of the region, for the first time.[2]

Q.   You also wanted to involve the schools in the region, didn't you?

A.   Yes! I felt the need of launching a broad program for young people in the schools and of outmoding the former practice of interrupting classes in order to take children to the theatre for a sort of noisy picnic. Students need to be prepared for the theatre; they need to know the history of the theatre, especially in those suburban schools far away from the center of theatrical activity. With the collaboration of a group of real theatrical creators, I sought to help these young people discover theatre as a means for losing inhibitions, as a noteworthy instrument for fantasies, and as a way of knowing one's own body on the level of instinctive gesticulation, which children possess but which the modern world is constantly repressing. This was a very important aspect of the work we undertook to do. At the same time, since we conceive theatre as a public service, that implied, for a city as large as Rome, the inclusion of experimental and research productions, which are, after all, basic to the make-up of Rome. As distinct from other Italian cities, Rome in recent years has been swarming with non-traditional theatrical groups who have unusual instinct and talent. From places such as cellars and other new theatrical spaces, they are sending us "off-Rome's" dramatic message, which is very important. It would

have been impossible to avoid establishing some kind of
relationship among these new forces, and we are giving
them the opportunity to express themselves, on an experimental and research basis.

Q.   It was also one of your original purposes to tour all of
Italy with your Company, to get people's reactions and
to consult with groups in each community in order to
know their theatrical preferences, etc. Were you able to
do all this, and with what results?

A.   Our gypsy quality is an unsuppressible reality, and it is
what took us last year on the trip through this long, difficult country that Italy is: long, because it is a long
boot, and difficult because it is so varied. From city to
city, within distances of just a few kilometers, there exist
more differences between Lucca, Grosseto and Arezzo
and between Siena and Florence than between Washing-
ton and Los Angeles. We heard one thing, basically: a
series of requests and intelligent observations by well-
disposed people, who are far superior to what we expected. We were convinced, in the end, that our splintered
structures are inadequate to reply to the requests of the
different societies that make up our country. It's strange,
but no matter what anyone says, the political authorities,
even in the small regional cities, have changed their attitude toward us — us, the working people of the theatre.
Another thing we felt was that Italy has a framework
that feels the pulse of certain needs, and that inevitably,
in time, things will develop in such a way that our activity will become more organic, less sporadic, and less in-
cidental throughout Italy. The thronging of the public
to the theatre — even a paying public — and the many
requests we have had from all over Italy, allow us to hope
that our activity will go in that direction. It's not that
the public wants to *study* theatre; it wants to *live* the
theatrical experience and place itself on a critical level
as well, in order to discuss and evaluate; it doesn't want
to express the enthusiasm of the bull-ring vis-à-vis the
theatre.

Q.   Are you satisfied with the choice of the Argentina
Theatre as the official seat of the Theatre of Rome?

A.   Given the nature of the Argentina Theatre —nineteenth century style, with boxes, conceived as an opera house where, incidentally, *The Barber of Seville* was booed — the main thing was to use it as a showplace but continue to search desperately for new theatrical spaces more suited to the development of a modern dramaturgy, or if this wasn't possible, to undo the lay-out and the architecture of the Argentina, the way Luchino Visconti did for Pinter's *Old Times:* he put the actors' zone of action in the center of the orchestra, making a sort of ring, surrounded by the public, with the spectators' stand on the stage. All of this was accomplished in the course of a season marked by improvisation on the spur of the moment, because I was named Director of the Theatre in early August and in the space of twenty days I had to outline a program. In those twenty days, I drew up a program that in some respects unfolded exactly as planned, but then it underwent changes during the course of the season. Changes that I must say were positive ones in the sense that they were shots that struck the bull's eye.

    At the end of the 1972-73 season began a period of reflection, and on the basis of the preceding experiences we began preparing the new 1973-74 season. Obviously every theatre is basically in the image and likeness of its Director. Every theatrical house has always mirrored its Artistic Director, or Director, or *Sovraintendente.* It is inconceivable to relate theatre to concepts of hospitality, or rented rooms, or hotel managers. It is imperative that all the risks, all the adventures, and all the dangers connected with a theatre reflect the person who directs it. I am much more an artistic director *(regista)* than a theatre director *(direttore di teatro)* in the German sense of the word, although even in Germany today we are witnessing the fact that many an *oberintendant* is being replaced by an artistic director who puts his own mark on the theatre. Clearly, the world of the artistic director and his way of conceiving theatrical action must be reflected in the functioning of this theatre. Despite all the limitations, defects, dangers and adventures connected with this theatre, my basic interests and efforts are aimed at discovering a new relationship with the public, which is revived each time it comes into contact with the theatrical fact, optimistically speaking. It is my aim to give to this theatrical fact—to the theatrical event—all its importance as an escape from all forms of theatrical demagogy or populism, yet at the same time to find, in this desperate tension caused by contact, communication and relation, the sources of a new, real, popular theatre for the future. The Argentina Theatre, as a theatrical instrument, because of its architectonic structure, is a rather dangerous and inhibiting instrument. In my opinion, it is necessary to maintain our showplace activity and hospitality at the Argentina, but to branch out simultaneously into new forms of theatrical space. We need to pierce the diaphragm between the scenic arch of the traditional stage and the often inert orchestra, which is the damnation of the contemporary theatre.

Q.   Will you tell us about your open-air production last season of *Life and Death of Cola di Rienzo?*

A.   It is really an exciting experience because Enzo Siciliano's text is built on a typically Roman character—a Roman tribune—who is Mussolini to a letter, from certain points of view. Thanks to Glauco Mauri's interpretation, it was a highly critical presentation that constantly grazed the grotesque or self-irony. There was a tremendous public turnout in the piazzas of the region: Anagni, Tarquinia, Tuscania, Viterbo and Civitavecchia, due in part, of course — I have no illusions — to the fact that there was no entrance fee. But that's one of our duties. In ancient Greece, at the time of Pericles, not only was theatre free, but spectators even received some form of compensation from the government for having left their work in order to attend a performance.

Q.   How do Italians react to the theatre of the absurd, the theatre of cruelty, and other forms of contemporary theatre that have had such impact in France?

A.   I think that, even though it has come about a little later than in other social contexts and collectivities, the end has finally come of purely commercial plays and naturalist theatre in Italy. My inaugural presentation— *Beckett '73,* composed of *Krapp's Last Tape, Act Without Words,* and *Not I* — at the new little Flaiano Theatre[3] — was such a tremendous success that we will repeat it next season for two months. This indicates a deep interest in — if we want to label them thus — the theatre of the absurd or the theatre of cruelty. No matter what is said about the modern Italian, I think the Italian imagination has behind it a tradition of the real Renaissance man's intelligence and fantasy. When conditions are favorable, the Italian can transpose himself to the level of fantasy and he is not on the level of realism, with which other countries have too conveniently labelled Italy.

Q.　What are your reactions to the Living Theatre? to Grotowski?

A.　The Living Theatre was for us a sort of contagion, in the sense that it set in motion a facile germination of followers and imitators of the Living Theatre style throughout Italy. But the Living Theatre had sprung from a reality profoundly different from our own. Its tour of Italy aroused an enthusiastic reception, and this was immediately followed by a series of bad imitations by people who had not assimilated the real lesson of the Living Theatre from all points of view and particularly from the point of view of theatrical research and the personal morality of the members of the group. Instead, through snobbishness, poor imitations were made of badly digested teachings.

　　Grotowski, on the other hand, has provoked more serious reactions, perhaps because he is closer to the spiritual and religious sensitivities of certain Italians. I think that Grotowski — for me, at least— has much more meaning than the Living Theatre. His experiments are for the most part inimitable, but the indications that he gives us after deep research are, in my opinion, more important and less marginal than those of the Living Theatre.

Q.　What will you be directing for the Theatre of Rome's 1973-74 season?

A.　Besides the carry-over from last year of the Beckett '73 festival, I'll be directing two new foreign plays during the 1973-74 season. The first is by an author who has come to the public attention only in the last two years as a true revelation re-discovered: Odön von Horvàth. He was born in Fiume, made his career in Middle Europe —Austria-Hungary and Germany— and died in Paris at the age of thirty-five. He is the author of a series of extraordinarily beautiful and interesting plays, produced during the period between the last of Schnitzler and the beginning of Brecht. I will direct, for the first time in Italy, his extraordinary *Casimir and Caroline* — a love story that unfolds in the midst of the Oktoberfest in Munich in 1932, just on the eve of the advent of Nazism in Germany. The second play I will direct is, once again, by an author who will be presented for the first time in Italy. It's *Divine Words (Divinas Palabras),* the masterpiece of that extraordinary Spanish poet, Ramón de Valle Inclàn. These two plays, then, will be presented for the first time in Italy, in Italian, by an Italian theatre. But I won't put them on at the Argentina. I'll stage them in a large circus somewhere on the outskirts of Rome.

Q.   Are there significant differences between Northern and Southern Italians, theatrically speaking?

A.   It's strange, but Northern Italy, from the point of view of passion for the theatre, receptivity and interest, is becoming lazier than the South. Strangely, the public in a city such as Bologna, which up to a few years ago was considered one of the liveliest and involved audiences, we now find to be lazy patrons, and the same is true for other cities. Perhaps it's because the preliminary exposure of performances, actors, directors, etc. in the North of Italy is undergoing the same changes that have occurred in advertising: to market a given canned product, you need an advertising budget and newspaper campaigns. South of the Apennines, on the other hand, there is still a certain freshness of receptivity by the public. Contact with the Southern audience is much more immediate and less affected by this preliminary publicity and this advertising that has become necessary in the North. Naturally, this puts a heavy responsibility on those who handle preliminary advertising — advertising also in the sense of preparation on the editorial, journalistic, cultural, and other levels. The public North of the

Apennines is more swayed and more swayable, more easily influenced and easier to copy, so it is already more predisposed, because certain levers have been manipulated, than the public South of the Apennines where, instead, there is a freshness of contact which is more old-fashioned, if you will, but more reasonable in a certain way. There are reasons for conceiving theatrical halls in a given way, for drawing up theatrical schedules in another way, for theatre becoming pure entertainment under certain life conditions and active, cultural participation under other conditions. There are so many reasons: price-politics, relations with students, etc. But one thing is clear today, and that is that theatres are getting to resemble more and more factories that turn out certain types of products. This is much truer today than ten years ago. Now it's a question of competing in marketing research.

Q.   Do young people react to the theatre in about the same way, regardless of which region of Italy they come from?

A.   Young Italians are all quite similar: they are interested and provoked in the same measure by the theatrical experience, whether it be in the North, South or Center of Italy. It is clear — and I am certain of this— that the future of our Italian theatre lies in the schools. The schools must teach theatre, must discover persons who will become actors and spectators, and must involve them in the absolutely unique adventure that theatre is.

Q.   Which contemporary dramatists—Italian or foreign—do you consider most highly, and why?

A.   It's so very difficult to say! Beckett, whom I consider one of the most extraordinary writers for the theatre and not only theatre; Tom Stoppard, whose *Rosencrantz and Guildenstern* I've done; Harold Pinter, whose *The Homecoming* I would have loved to do since I consider it a masterpiece of the contemporary theatre. But obviously I'm missing a lot of others; these are just the first who come to mind. I am convinced that the only possible way to judge a work is by our enthusiasm with respect to certain reactions. Gone are the days, at least in Italy, when we could presume to feed the public with theatrical productions according to our own desires. The number of failures experienced by impresarios, directors and producers now in Italy — when only a few years ago it was presumed that the public would accept any fancy dish you put in front of it—demonstrates that it is a risk each time and you never know how it will turn out. The only way to evaluate a work is according to your own sensitivities, interest and enthusiasm, and your own faith and commitment to a certain text that you want to stage.

Q.   Your office[4] is overflowing with Goldoni volumes. Which is your favorite Goldoni comedy and why?

A.   Well, *The Mistress of the Inn* comes first. I consider it one of Goldoni's masterpieces, and its modernity is upsetting if your consider certain characters, especially Mirandolina, who is a real, true business woman. Then, besides this one, many others; but one that I would love to stage and that is little known is one of Goldoni's early works: *A Man of the World.* It is just the vehicle for a young, disillusioned character, cynically Casanovian—not on the scale of a Don Giovanni but rather at the level of melancholy disenchantment with the world. It's completely modern.

Q.   Will you say something about the financial situation of the Theatre of Rome? What are your plans and hopes for the future?

A.   The closing of the 1972-73 season was in some respects exceptionally positive, in the sense that income and subscriptions were far higher than expected. But, of course, expenses, too, were higher than expected due to increases in costs and certain budget items like transportation, overtime for actors, and missing or inadequate construction in a theatre that had remained unused for such a long time. So the view of the final balance sheet was very positive. Naturally, to get the pilot experiments we were talking about earlier to go in the right direction, we need more financial support from the Ministry on the one hand and from the Local Administrations on the other. I

must say that, here in Rome, there have been some absolutely enlightened people: the authorities in Rome's
Local Administration have never denied me help and
encouragement in my activity as Director of a theatre,
and I hope this will continue. The things that remain
for us to do are undoubtedly beyond our strength — not
physical but economic strength. Unfortunately, we have
come to the realization, on the basis of our experiences,
that the society of Rome and the Lazio region requires
more than we are able to give. If we compare the funds
allotted to an important Theatre like the Theatre of
Rome by the Local Administration and by the Government, with the funds allotted certain State Theatres in
Germany, the comparison is derisory. We receive much,
much less, and we do much, much more. There is not a
shadow of a doubt that this is true.

I hope it is obvious that I have handled this year's
funds well. Despite what some petty, evil tongues may
say, I will say that I have handled them well, and the
proof of this is that we have received an increase in
ministerial contributions in recognition of our efforts.
Hopefully, the ill-disposed critics who have been firing at
us all last year, hoping to send us to an early death, will
now keep silent. But all of that is part of the difficulties
connected with the theatre.

[1] The old Stabile Theatre of Rome had been inactive for several
years, limiting itself to receiving traditional companies on the
stage of its Argentina Theatre.

[2] The Theatre of Rome's decentralization plan offered a sub-
scription series in ten minor cities of the Lazio region: Tarquinia, Frosinone, Tuscania, Civitavecchia, Anagni, Rieti, Gaeta,
Terni, Latina, and Viterbo. All seats sold at a single price — five
hundred lire (about eighty-five cents). The repertoire included

Brecht's *Mother Courage,* Goldoni's *The Lovers,* Euripides' *Medea,* Shakespeare's *Hamlet,* Pirandello's *Liolà,* and Enzo Siciliano's *Life and Death of Cola di Rienzo.*

[3] Formerly the Arlecchino Theatre, adjacent to the Argentina, and renamed in honor of Ennio Flaiano, a well-known Italian journalist and dramatist. Since the Flaiano Theatre has only 183 seats, it is better suited than the Argentina, which has about 1,000 seats to certain types of productions.

[4] Mr. Enriquez' office, in the Argentina Theatre, is reputed to be Cesare Borgia's study.

FRANCO FANO

Interviewer's Note:

Drama critic Franco Fano contributes to numerous cultural and theatrical publications. He is a keenly critical observer and commentator of the contemporary Italian theatrical scene.

Q.   Would you sketch a panorama of the modern Italian theatre as you see it?

A.   During the 1960s, there was a "boom" in the Italian theatre; it was a period of renewed activity in the dramatic world, and a time of great public enthusiasm for the theatre.[1] It lasted six or seven years — perhaps less but not more. It seemed as though people had suddenly re-discovered the theatre, in a new dimension, different from before — let's say from before the war,. from the period of Fascism. Before and during the war, theatre was generally considered by a public unaccustomed to other concepts to be an escape, a diversion. So people went to the theatre to be entertained. This was the era of the *pochade,* where a lot of French plays were performed, but Italianized for political reasons — the foolish political reasons of the time. The theatre, then, was entertaining, but had no significance. Among the light Italian authors were Dino Falconi and Oreste Biancoli. Carlo Veneziani was even better known, but his plays, too, contained very little that was meaningful. The range of plays at the *pochades* extended from Feydeau to the French classics. Then, suddenly, partly because of a maturing process on various levels of conscience between the public and the theatrical world, partly because some individuals took the offensive, after the war the theatre became committed, resulting in greater interest on the part of the public. So, we have reached the end of the 1950s and the beginning of the 60s, when this explosion, this "boom" took place, thanks to the activity of certain men like Vittorio Gassman, for example, who undertook to establish a popular theatre of commitment. He tried to bring the classics to the widest general public. Even his classical Greek productions were presented in a modernized version, easy and accessible to the general public. The famous Circus Theatre, which originated in Milan and then came to Rome, failed miserably because Gassman was not successful in getting sufficient funds for it. Naturally, a theatre that attracts to a circus tent every evening a thousand people who pay only 200 lire (about 30 cents) cannot be self-sufficient because obviously the tent, the lights, the personnel and the actors cost a great deal of money. So the experiment failed. But not because it wasn't worthwhile or because of lack of public support; it failed because Gassman, with the intention of creating an authentic popular theatre from the point of view of both content and policy, charged only 200 lire a seat. Naturally, the theatre could not survive. Exigencies are what they are.

Q.   Were there other important theatrical groups at this time?

A.   Yes, there were other important companies, like the one directed by Giancarlo Sbragia, and the Company of the Young: Giorgio De Lullo, Rossella Falk, Romolo Valli and Elsa Albani; and others, but I cannot name them all now. In any case, these companies strove to contribute to the renewal of the theatre, re-discovering Italian, foreign, ancient and classical texts, but above all, introducing modern and contemporary authors. They tried to co-ordinate their efforts with other attempts to popularize the theatre, but they nevertheless remained travelling companies that performed in theatres where ticket sales were remunerative. It was in this context that the Company of the Young brought about the re-discovery of Pirandello; they presented Pirandello, who up to that time was unknown or not sufficiently known to the Italian public, in a more understandable way, more acceptable to the public.

Q.   How do you explain the necessity of a "re-discovery" of
      Pirandello in Italy?

A.   When Pirandello was first presented in Italy in the 1920s,
      all his works were hissed and whistled at, starting with his
      characters, because they were portrayed bombastically.
      Inasmuch as Pirandello's theatre is difficult— it is a the-
      atre of introspection, and not within everyone's reach—
      it was only natural that audiences would not be touched
      by that kind of portrayal. Subsequently, however, there
      was a broadening of the public's cultural horizons —
      something inevitable after a war and especially after a war
      such as ours—which opened and channeled itself towards
      completely new perspectives. Now people knew a little
      more about psychoanalysis and had done some other
      reading, so Pirandello no longer was the madman. He be-
      came a worthwhile author, and even in the theatre he be-
      came more comprehensible. Now he was liked, and there
      was a Pirandello "boom." As a matter of fact, the Com-
      pany of the Young made famous their rendition of *Six
      Characters In Search of an Author,* which they performed
      unforgettably here in Rome. Later, Giorgio Strehler pre-
      sented other versions of Pirandello — *The Game of the
      Powerful,* for example—in a different version from his
      1932 production: updated, more modern, more compre-
      hensible this time.

Q.   What was the role of the Stabile Theatres during this
      epoch?

A.   To the activity of these pioneers such as Gassman and to
      the efforts of intelligent theatre people such as the Com-
      pany of the Young, Sbragia and some others, we must
      add the Stabile Theatres, which are like a public service.
      They are a cultural institution at the service of the public,
      and defined, in a political sense, by the same standards as
      a public transportation system — that is, a theatre which
      is necessary, useful, and easily accessible to all, from both
      the cultural and economic point of view. Practically
      every city has its Stabile Theatre. The first was a famous
      one—the best-known —the Piccolo of Milan, founded by
      Paolo Grassi, who is presently its Director, and who was
      joined, as co-Artistic Director, by Giorgio Strehler, one of

our outstanding directors. To these men we owe not only the formulation of Italy's theatrical policy but also the introduction of Brecht who, before Grassi and Strehler, was almost completely unknown in Italy. They gave us unforgettable productions of Brecht, from *The Threepenny Opera* to *Arturo Ui*. Strehler subsequently put on much Goldoni, Pirandello, etc.

The Stabile Theatre is financed by public contributions and government subsidies that are intended as a form of encouragement. The municipality contributes money derived from taxes on municipal services. In addition, the theatre brings in money and one like Milan's has considerable income from related activities such as lectures, debates, publications, etc. So it is not totally passive — it is passive, but at least has an autonomous life of its own, in part. Other important Stabile Theatres functioning at about the same time as Milan's were the Stabile of Genoa, directed by Luigi Squarzina as Artistic Director and Ivo Chiesa as Administrative Director. These are two great men of the theatre, on a level equal to Strehler and Grassi. Then there was the Stabile of Turin, a big, important theatre for which I worked as a consultant. The history of this Theatre is interesting because, more than any other, it performed in the provinces. It brought its services throughout the province of Piedmont, which is vast. The Turin Stabile Theatre was also the first to experiment with theatre in the schools, that is, theatre for children. I'm still speaking now of those years of the "boom," from about 1958 to 1965 or 1966, *grosso modo.*

All the Stabile Theatres have similar statutes; they are all conceived along the same lines; and they all are required to bring theatre to the provincial centers which are generally deprived of any theatrical experience. They are supposed to bring good plays, plays for young people, plays for the schools, and charge very low admission prices. Some theatres do this, but some don't. Some do quite a bit of it, and others much less. Some do it well and some do it poorly. The example of the Stabile of Turin is unique: it brought theatre to the provinces in an outstanding manner. In fact, I remember having seen Giulio Bosetti in a performance with the Stabile of Turin, which at that time was directed by Gianfranco De Bosio, an excellent Director and now Artistic Director for the Arena of Verona since he has given up the theatre. Bosetti was doing Goldoni — I think it was *Harlequin, Servant of Two Masters* — in a revised, modernized version, in the small town of Alba, near Turin. The audience of young children thoroughly enjoyed Goldoni, who is not an easy author by any means. They understood the hidden meanings in the play. And when they were later interviewed at school for a television program, and were given a composition assignment at school on the subject of Harlequin's meanings, these children demonstrated an exceptional maturity. They had understood the entire play, which is only to say that if things are explained well to children, in a way suited to their age, they understand, and you can construct in them not only a general cultural foundation but also a love for the theatre. For when there is love for the theatre, there is theatre, and when that love does not exist, there is no theatre.

Franco Enriquez was also part of that small group of committed theatre people of the time. He was the Director of the famous Company of Four: Valeria Moriconi, Glauco Mauri, Emanuele Luzzati and himself. His contributions to the theatre are eminent. For example, he re-discovered Shakespeare in a new dimension. He made Shakespeare relevant to today's world. He gave us Shakespeare's philosophy and his way of looking at the world in a modern form. Shakespeare, like all classical writers, dresses his characters in the costume of the sixteenth century or other epochs close to his time and presents situations which are not contemporary situations. A very banal example: Shakespeare's Prince rides a horse; today's Prince travels by jet. The feelings in Shakespeare's characters, however, are the same for all times: love, hatred, rivalry, evil, etc. These are feelings that have the same value now as then, except that they are expressed differently. So what Enriquez and others of his calibre have done is to render in a contemporary style the expressions of these sentiments, thereby bringing Shakespeare's theatre close to today's spectator and allowing him to enjoy and profit more from the meaning of Shakespearian drama, even though the scenario and the costumes remain those of times past. The sentiments are frequently rendered more comprehensible by free interpretation of the texts. Contemporary directors have re-read Shakespeare critically— and in this respect Enriquez has been outstanding. And in the interpretation of Rosalind, for example, Valeria Moriconi outdid herself.

Q.   The revival of the theatre lasted, then, only until the mid-sixties. How do you account for the ending of the "boom"?

A.   As I said earlier, where there is no love for the theatre, there can be no theatre. As a matter of fact, in Italy, where love for the theatre often is nothing but middle-class snobbishness, there is no theatre. The "boom" lasted only a short time; it was followed by a sharp drop in theatre attendance; today the theatres are almost empty; the theatre. is languishing because it lacks bite and has no impetus such as the re-discovery of the classics, or of Pirandello, etc. Various experiments have been made: there was, for example, an interesting Italian assimilation of England's Angry Young Men, of Pinter and others in his school, due to the fact that they were concerned with contemporary problems and, after the war, when people spoke of civilian recovery and moral reconstruction, that type of theatre had great appeal. Naturally, Pinter is completely outdated today. People would laugh if you tried to put on Pinter, because Pinter hasn't written anything new or, if he has, he has become so bourgeois that he no longer is relevant.
        Then there was the re-discovery of Ionesco and the theatre of the absurd. All of Ionesco's most important plays have been produced in Italy. Not like in Paris, of course, where *The Bald Soprano* played for eight years at La Huchette Theatre. This could never happen in Italy: the public is different; it has a different substratum. Rome has never been a cultural capital like Paris. There are historic reasons for this, which the sociologists and the philosophers can explain, but which go beyond the scope of our interest here, which is the theatre.

Q.   What is the attitude of the younger generation toward the theatre in Italy?

A.   The younger generation would be extremely interested in what theatre can offer, but since they were born in a completely different era and see things in a completely different way, you would have to give them a non-bourgeois theatre. In other words, they can't conceive of going to the theatre at nine o'clock in a dark suit and strutting around the lobby in order to be seen. That's not theatre for them. Theatre is something easily accessible, at convenient hours for those who work or study, and a place you go to without changing clothes. In Paris, for example, workers go to the Théâtre National Populaire in their overalls.

Q.   What did you think of *Hair?*

A.   It was meaningless. I had read the original text as well as the criticisms of the American, English, and French versions. I saw it performed first in Paris, then in Rome. The Italian version was extraordinarily chaste! Not only because the girls wore bras, but also because they cut out the strongest lines. I can understand that *Hair* represents a rupture with traditional theatre, and that it serves the purpose of opening up new dramatic horizons, but this is not what Italian youth is looking for. The public that went to see *Hair* was the same audience that buys pornographic magazines or those lovely drawing-room ladies that look like decadent exballerinas.

Q.   There has been some talk about a new revival of the Italian theatre in the early 1970s. Do you think it is in the making?

A.   Well, just take a look at the 1972-73 season: it was abysmal! Dramatic theatre has lost all contact with the public. Because of the lack of new texts dealing with today's problems, because of the lack of original ideas, which forces the theatre to fall back on the old repertories, and because of the obstinacy of social habits, the theatre has lost all cultural content and has become absolutely inadequate to the exigencies of an audience that is thirsting for debate and for democaracy. They say that today's confusion, disorder, and inability to escape infernal life correspond to man's inability to escape his moral disorder, his confusion, and his spiritual near-

sightedness. Probably this is ture. But it also is true that
there have been pitifully few enlightened reactions to the
situation in the last few years in the theatre. All these
old, worn out plays that continue to be performed without any attempt to make them relevant! And whatever
classics are chosen are done so in a spirit of mental lazi-
ness and with sheer immaturity! The 1972-73 season, in
sum, was notorious for the absence of practically all the
most important Italian actors, directors and producers
from the theatrical scene. But I must admit that there
were a few good things: *Much Ado About Nothing* at
Rome's Valle Theatre, and a decidedly nonconventional
Inspector General by Mario Missiroli. Blok's *Balangacik,*
offered by Daniele Constantini on the little stage of the
Flaiano Theatre, was a serious attempt to reach a new
cultural level. [2]At the Quirino Theatre, another Shakespeare work, *A Midsummer Night's Dream,* directed by
Egisto Marcucci, contained an original social impact and
highly imaginative fantasy. Pirandello's *The Pleasure of
Honesty,* starring Salvo Randone, was outstanding for the
actor's rigorous interpretation and his measured exalta-
tion of the text's humanism. I must also mention Luigi
Squarzina's production of *Mother Courage* with Lina
Volonghi at the Eliseo Theatre, and Goldoni's *Mistress of
the Inn* with Anna Maria Guarnieri, directed by Mario
Missiroli, once again. And, at Rome's Argentina Theatre,
under the artistic directorship of Franco Enriquez,
Pirandello's *Liolà,* directed and performed by Turi Ferro,
Brecht's *The Good Woman of Setsuan,* directed by Benno
Besson, Goldoni's *The Lovers,* and Valeria Moriconi's
intelligent interpretation of Euripides' *Medea* — all bore
the inimitable mark of Enriquez' talent.

      This, however, is not enough for a theatrical
season. We must react against the crisis that has taken
hold of the theatre—and not yet released its grip—by
unlocking the feelings that torment people today. The
public wants to be faced with genuinely human perspectives. The theatre must offer ideas, proposals, or at
least the opportunity for useful debate on contemporary
moral and civil problems.

      The Stabile Theatre of Catania is the only one
that operates seriously and meaningfully today. It
centers on the initiative and activity of Turi Ferro, who is

a great actor and who has also directed plays. He is
highly capable, and a first rate man. He has worked
with Strehler in Milano, and also for television. The
Catania Stabile Theatre has produced many important
and worthwhile things. Its Sicilian repertory is especially
notable. They have done *Cavalleria Rusticana* and a lot
of Pirandello. The Sicilian repertory responds to the
needs of the conservative public there, which doesn't
like innovations very much, doesn't believe easily in
futurism, nor in burning matters, nor in ruptures with
traditional works. Just imagine trying to bring Brecht
to the Sicilians! I'm sorry to have to say this, because I
am an Italian, but our country is severely handicapped,
especially from the cultural point of view. We are not a
country; we are ten, twenty countries. What affinities
can there be between a Sicilian and a Venetian? None!
The Venetian loves Goldoni; the Sicilian doesn't even
understand Goldoni. Not only does he express himself
in different words, but he expresses different sentiments.
The Sicilian is the man who kills for honor; the Venetian,
on the other hand, tolerates a seventeen-year old girl
going off with the boys, and no-one will refer to her as a
prostitute. They are completely different. They have
nothing in common. Which theatre could possibly suit
both one and the other? Certainly, there will be progress,
but it is slow—very slow. And you have to add to ethical
explanations questions of politics and selfish interest as
well. We do not live in a free world. We do not live in a
democratic world....

Q. Would you tell us more about dialect theatre in Italy?

A. There is the Sicilian dialect theatre, but it has almost
completely disappeared. There are Nino Martoglio's and
Angelo Musco's plays, which are put on from time to
time by the Stabile of Catania, or by small, amateur
Sicilian groups dedicated to the theatre and who sometimes put on a rather good performance. But even that is
falling out of style. Then there's Goldoni in Venetian;
and some Genovese dialect theatre. Roman dialect
theatre scarcely exists any more — there are some worn
out plays with no cultural importance. In Naples, there
is Eduardo De Filippo's theatre — a cultural theatre —

which stages Eduardo's comedies interpreted by others.
This, too, is disappearing gradually. During the 1972-73
season, for example, there were no performances because
they are not remunerative. The group prefers to make a
film or a special television show. Theatre doesn't allow
them to earn enough any more — and they do have to
live! No one today is going to make such a sacrifice!
The man of the theatre, like everyone else, wants to buy
a villa, two cars, furs, etc.

Q.   So you are almost completely negative and pessimistic
       about the contemporary Italian theatre?

A.   Well, there was a serious attempt at revival, and it failed,
       mainly because the effort did not receive sufficient sup-
       port from the public and from existing social structures.
       There are no supporting structures in Italy, so it's not
       easy to have theatre. There are too many selfish inter-
       ests. Of course, there are problems everywhere in the
       world, but Sir Laurence Olivier is in the theatre with the
       support of the state, and he can do whatever he chooses.
       There are different mentalities and different systems.
       Here in Italy, the theatre has not found a suitable struc-
       tural foundation. So that noble and generous attempt
       on the part of the theatre world to bring about a revival
       of drama in Italy lacked public and government support,
       and now those pioneers are tired. They try to keep
       afloat, but their initiative is slackening. There are no
       organic programs, and no clear roadmarks. They don't
       know too well what the public wants; or, rather, they
       know that they should give the public certain things,
       but they don't do so because it's not convenient. They
       know that it is extremely hard to get a vast public to ap-
       preciate good things, so they prefer to compromise by
       producing one good play and ten bad ones — that is,
       one with true, cultural, authentic content and then
       escapist plays that attract either because of the type of
       comedy or the name of the artist. For example, Alberto
       Lupo or Alida Valli are successful in the theatre because
       they are the "pretty people" of television. They are not
       dramatic actors; they have nothing to communicate from
       the stage. Nothing is really going on now on the stage:
       it has been years since we have seen something meaning-

ful. We go to the theatre today just to see these people talking and moving about. We sit for two hours, maybe we laugh, or maybe we reflect on certain life situations. But that's not theatre. Theatre means educating, leading the public forward on a very specific path, guiding it by means of organic discussion. A theatrical troupe, in my opinion and, I think, in the opinion of others, should be able to say: "All right! Let's concentrate now on the subject of honesty. People today have become dishonest, and we want to talk about honesty. So let's find a certain number of dramatic works—scripts that debate the theme of honesty — pro or con. Then let's try to establish a dialogue with the audience in an attempt to find out why we are dishonest." What I mean to say is that the theatre should offer ideas, must open a dialogue, and possibly find answers to the problems facing society today. These answers may not be the definitive ones. No one is a prophet. But attempts should be made to find answers. When such discussion is lacking, when these moral values and these goals are lacking, theatre has no purpose, just as literature and music would be purposeless without them. That is the definition of culture. Culture is not the putting together of something to show people for the price of a ticket!

---

[1] Government support for the theatre was granted in the 1965-69 Five-Year Economic Development draft plan. Interviewer's note.

[2] See interview with Daniele Costantini, below.

ARNOLDO FOÀ

Interviewer's Note:

A dramatic and film actor, Arnoldo Foà was born in Ferrara on January 24, 1916 and studied in Florence. He made his theatrical debut in 1938 as the Sea Captain, Antonio, in Shakespeare's *Twelfth Night.* At the age of nineteen, he went to Rome and, contrary to his real inclinations, enrolled at the Experimental Center for Cinematography. He has acted in many films, but without total dedication to the medium. Between 1941 and 1956, Foà performed with various theatrical groups, and then formed his own company with three other actors. At the same time, he wrote his first play, *Good Evening, Ladies and Gentlemen (Signori, Buonasera),* which he himself directed at the Odeon Theatre in Milan on March 18, 1957. Although he performs extensively for radio, Foà is best known for his meditative insight into the character he portrays on stage, and for the dry modernity and sobriety of gesture and intonation in his dramatic renditions.

Q.   You say in the program notes (for Maurizio Costanzo's *Return Empty Bottles*) that the more proposals you get for Brechtian performances, the more you feel like acting slowly and calmly, simply and naturally, moderately and effectively. Will you explain this statement?

A.   What I mean is that Brecht's theatre is literary. Of course, it does require practice on the actors' part, but a practice that goes beyond what can be learned in school or from a technique. A technique can be mastered — which is a fascinating thing and maybe even an advantage for certain kinds of theatre, but not for *all* theatre. There cannot be the same form for all theatre. So gradually we lose the actors in their infinite possibilities. Actors who are limited to only one possibility cannot have the possibility of being naturalist actors too.

Q. In your opinion, does Maurizio Costanzo's *Return Empty
   Bottles treat a typically Italian contemporary problem or
   does it express something more universal? What are the
   problems facing Italians today for which the theatre
   might serve as a vehicle of expression?

A. In my opinion, the problems of Italians are the same as
   everyone else's problems. Every nation, every area of the
   world, every man has problems, and the theatre is able to
   describe all problems. In Costanzo's play, the problem of
   old age is just touched on. It is not a particularly Italian
   problem. It is a universal one, but it is just touched on
   lightly. It would seem that in America the problem of
   old people has assumed a strange quality: namely, old
   people live just like the young! We see them globe-
   trotting, dressed in the most unbelievable way, elderly
   women displaying nothing very desirable in their mini-
   skirts, paralytics and paraplegics (who in Italy probably
   wouldn't budge from their homes) on the go, moving
   about and travelling. I don't know whether it's the
   American pension system or the work they've done during their lifetime, or their capacity for economizing — the
   fact remains that as old people, they are able to live a life
   that perhaps they did not even live when they were
   young. I don't think this would be possible in Italy.
   At least it would be very difficult. Old Italians — old
   Europeans — tend to shut themselves up. I know that
   in the Soviet Union, too, much is being done for the old;
   schools are set up for them, and I think this is extremely
   utilitarian. Just last evening, I was reading about acu-
   puncture in a book by an American physician — an
   anesthetist, I think, whose name escapes me just now.
   He described a certain procedure in a 2,000 yer-old
   technique: if you don't feel well, get up, do certain
   calisthenics in accordance with prescribed principles,
   and when you are all perspired, sprinkle your body with
   rice, and you'll feel fine. I really believe this to be true.
   The old Italian generally neglects himself, no longer ex-
   ercises, and moves around very little. But apart from
   this, the universal problem of old age is posed by a longer
   lifespan. Surgery, penicillin and other drugs now combat

illnesses that formerly decimated the old. In times past, old people died of pneumonia. They just expected to die that way. To fall and break a hip and to die of penumonia were one and the same. Today, instead, one can break a hip and pneumonia does not necessarily have to set in. So, naturally, the world's population of oldsters is growing; population increases result not only from births but from an extended lifespan and a lower mortality rate.

Q.   Who, in your opinion, are the most important Italian dramatists?

A.   Certainly Peppino Patroni Griffi is one of the most important, from the point of view of language as well. I find Griffi's Italian to be very close to today's realities, and his theatre reflects a life which is really Italian. Another writer of considerable interest — a young man— is Renato Mainardi, who has not produced very much, but he, too, demonstrates a certain mastery in writing. And then, naturally, there is myself...but I won't talk about myself. I am less concerned with Italian problems than with universal ones. Another excellent theatrical writer is Natalia Ginzburg, who writes very well. Up to now, however, her production has been lean — just little tableaux, a one-act play, or two skimpy acts. She hasn't yet produced a real drama — and we're eagerly awaiting this. I don't know any other interesting Italian dramatic authors.

Q.   Have you ever performed in any of your own plays?

A.   Only two. A drama entitled *The Witness* and, before that, a satire of the Italian theatre as it was fifteen or twenty years ago— that is, a theatre that was tied to the apron strings of and sucked milk from "light" authors, (I don't want to mention any names) for whom going to see a play was synonymous with going to see nothing. These authors were able, however, to force the hand of the Ministry to the point that it became obligatory in Italy for acting companies to perform a certain percentage of Italian comedies — 50 per cent, I think — rather than the more favored, more important foreign comedies. So I satirized this situation, taking as my point of departure an imaginary Italian author who writes a French-type comedy and hands it to the actors, saying: "Perform it as one big laugh. But you must feel it!" The actors rebel, saying that they feel it *as Italians,* and there is nothing amusing in the comedy. Since it is a play about cuckoldry, Italians don't laugh. It's very hard to make them laugh about this subject; they may pretend to laugh, but they don't succeed. At a certain point in the play, the author comes on stage to ask the protagonists how long they have been lovers. The actor replies that he doesn't know. Two young men come out on stage from the respective bedrooms of the two daughters of the house, followed by the daughters who see their mother in the embrace of her lover. Now the mother can no longer reproach her daughters, and the daughters suffer horrible grief because they have seen their mother with her lover. The author-actor says: "This is comic!" But where is the comedy in all this? How could you possibly render it comic? As a matter of fact, the "comedy" ends with a pistol-shot. No one knows which of the three women has shot herself offstage. The three men only remain on stage. Each of the three men, however, is perfectly aware that any one of the three women had every reason to commit suicide. The unsolved tragedy ends with the humorous: "Ladies and gentlemen, dinner is served!" The pistol-shot was completely unexpected by the author-actor, who onstage says: "But I didn't write that!" Because it was a sound, and naturally he didn't *write* it!

Q.   Italian theatrical tastes seem to tend more toward the classics and toward foreign dramatists than toward Italian contemporary authors. Why?

A.   Well, a little because we are a people who generally denigrate ourselves. But I think this is true practically everywhere. (No man is a prophet in his own land, goes the Latin proverb.) In Italy, writing is considered a somewhat domestic affair. What I mean is that we always prefer to read things that stun our imagination, things that go beyond our everyday reality. In a sense, this is in accordance with the general public taste for knowing

"other things," things not domestic, for one knows
one's house all too well. Other people's problems are,
without a doubt, newer and more interesting. Moreover, writers in Italy write for the stage revues, which
are almost always about things Italian. They are the same
writers; they don't change their writing style, but they
just stress the comic instead of the serious....

Certainly, when I read Shakespeare, in all his
manifestations, be they comic or tragic, he is totally
fascinating. For me, all writers are classic. I never consider the classical writer as a classical writer. A classic
is classic insofar as at a given moment the problem under
consideraton by the author becomes necessarily and
ineluctably so important, so universal, that the work
becomes classical. When the work was written, it was not
a classic. When one writes, one is not a classical writer;
one is just any contemporary.

Q.   How do Italians react to avant-garde theatre? Are Arrabal, Beckett, or even Ionesco appreciated in Italy?

A.   Yes. The are appreciated. They fulfill their function.
But at this point I must say that I think the Italian people
— I am speaking of the theatrical public —thirst for simple things, and that is why I chose Maurizio Costanzo's
play, which you saw this evening. Even though I am a
man of the theatre, I am also a man of politics. Not that
I am engaged in politics, but I am a political creature, as
we all are. So, during the day, I have an infinite number
of preoccupations, whether it be the war in Vietnam or
the Middle East. The newspapers keep me aware of the
infinite number of serious problems in the world. In the
evening, therefore, I would like to be distracted. That is,
when I have finished my day of work, of preoccupations,
of writing, etc., I need distraction. Often I prefer to go
to see a light film or play rather than anything heavy,
because already, during the day, I have had my fill of
drama. And perhaps the Italian theatrical public has
reached just this point of saturation. That's why "difficult" theatre... —Ionesco transports you onto another
level, but his anti-bourgeois messages still maintain a
tonality of lightness, but Beckett is difficult. He is much
more serious. Beckett involves you with all your might.

You cannot listen to him without effort. You really have to make an effort to listen to his plays. And this year, I simply wanted to unburden my soul with a light comedy.

Q.   Have you anything to say about dialect theatre in Italy? Is it disappearing? And if so, will it be a loss, in your opinion, or do you think that Italian language and art should be standardized?

A.   I couldn't say that dialect theatre is part of our folklore; that wouldn't be right. Italian dialect theatre has assumed, over the ages, the role of the chorus in the theatre. There has been Venetian theatre, which even though in dialect was a great theatre. There is Goldoni... Presently, the highest expression of dialect theatre is that of Eduardo De Filippo, whose works are in dialect but are universal. Probably he will be considered a classic in the future. Dialect expression has the advantage of an immediacy which literary, grammatical Italian sometimes does not have. Italian, like many other Mediterranean tongues, is anchored in rigid grammatical rules — and this is in absolute contrast with the spoken language. Moreover, the elongated geographic shape of Italy has divided us linguistically, into four stocks: Northern Italian, which can be subdivided; Central Italian; and Southern Italian. It is difficult to create one language which would be the same for all four groups —five, in fact: Northern Italy is subdivided into Liguria, Lombardy, and Venice, where three completely different languages are spoken. So it is very difficult to find a language or to create one that could be assimilated by all. We are awaiting the time — which will necessarily come because of radio and television—when all Italians will speak Italian correctly. Obviously, that time has not yet come because if you go to Sicily you are sometimes not understood. Or to Calabria, where you are not understood if you speak pure Italian. But it would be a pity to eliminate dialect theatre; it would be wrong to say that it does not represent a form of art; it would also be wrong, however, to say that only dialects can produce art forms. Art is wherever we find it. It may be that tomorrow a Genovese will be born who will write marvelous comedies in his dialect, so that the

language will immediately take the ascendancy. What I
am saying is that the Genovese dialect could achieve
supremacy. Just as when Dante wrote the *Divine Comedy* and the Italian language was subsequently based on
Dante Alighieri, who was Tuscan. Once, during a lecture,
I jokingly used the words in the *Inferno* of Farinata degli
Uberti:

> "O Tosco che per la città del foco
> vivo ten vai così parlando onesto,
>
> ....
>
> La tua loquela ti fa manifesto
> di quella nobil patria natio..."

> "O Tuscan! thou, who through that city of fire
> alive art passing, so discreet of speech,
>
> ....
>
> Thy utterance declares the place of thy nativity
> to be that noble land..."

This means that Dante spoke Tuscan. Written Italian
remained, but he spoke Tuscan, and the language was
born there. Our Italian languae was born in Sicily. The
language of Ferrara is Italian, but it all began in Sicily.
The earliest Italian literature, the first poems, have their
origins in Sicily. So you see it is hard to say what is good
and what is bad. Art finds its paths where it will find
them.

Q.   Are there differences between Northern and Southern
theatrical tastes?

A.   I have been in the theatre for thirty years, and I can say
there are tremendous differences, but I have yet to understand of what they consist. Generally speaking, the
Southern theatrical public prefers drama, while the
Northerners prefer comedy — this is *grosso modo*. One
proof of this is that in Milan, for some years now, they
have been training actors who are not actors but manual
laborers. They put on comedies in the Milanese dialect.
I have never seen them, so I can't judge them, but I know
they put on simple little comedies which are very amusing. There are no women in their ranks; men play the fe-
male parts. They extemporise, somewhat in the tradition

of the *commedia dell'arte* of old, using no written texts but rather creating as they go along. In times past, Milan used to be the testing-ground for all plays, serious or comic. Today, however, comedies are predominant in the North and serious plays in the South. I have never understood, though, why a comedy succeeds in Milan and is a flop in Rome, or vice versa. Generally speaking, if the play originates in Rome, it fares badly in Milan; if it originates in Milan, it fares badly in Rome. I don't know what it depends on. I can't explain the reasons for the difference.

Q.   What do you see in the future for the Italian theatre?

A.   At this time, I really don't know what to say about the future of the Italian theatre. All I know is that the theatre is moribund but never dies. It always seems to be on the verge of dying, but never does. It needs a spiritual struggle to engage it — that is, satire, which is the most beautiful form of theatre. From Aristophanes to Plautus, satire has always been the most lively and the most effective form of theatre, and the one that offers man the greatest possibilities of expressing himself in the face of stifled freedom or unjust laws. Naturally, this does not occur in Shakespeare, because he rose in all his grandeur to accomplish the same thing —we don't know against whom! Because basically, in Shakespeare's time, freedom was not stifled. Yes! Life was stifling, but I don't think that in his day there were many political movements. I don't know. I must admit that I don't know too much about that period of English history.

It is hard to say what will happen in the future. Today, it would be difficult to speak of an Italian theatre and its position on the international theatrical scene. We can speak of the importance of the Italian movies on the world scene, but as for theatre I would say that we haven't much to offer, just as France hasn't much to offer nowadays — just like England, and just like America. We are all impoverished—I don't know why—despite the succession and alternance of plays on the boards. I might say parenthetically that I had received a request from a Greek troupe that wanted to stage one of my plays. They returned the script to me, laughingly, saying that they could never put it on because it satirized a dictator. And so my play was never performed.

Q.   What are your political ideas?

A.   I am a Socialist. I don't think communism can offer a wide scope of freedom — or at least that's how it looks. Socialism takes man's nature into account, whereas communism considers it to be perfect. I think man is perfectible, but not perfect; that man tends toward honesty but that this propensity toward honesty, in practice...— well, man is man. So he must be accepted with his defects, which are also defects of affection really — a father expects more from his own son than he does from someone else's son. This is a fact of human nature; we can't get away from it. We are made that way. So socialism, I believe, is something attainable because it respects everyone—at least to a certain point. Communism, on the other hand, strives to level everyone. I don't think that can ever be achieved, because in my opinion the absolute levelling of mankind is impossible, and the imposition of an absolute levelling desired by a government will lead inevitably to revolutions.

Q.   Why is there no politico-satirical theatre in Italy?

A.   There is a secondary form of politico-satirical theatre: the little "boîtes" or "tabarins", where you will find very good actors. It's a rich and lively theatre, here in Rome and also in Milan and Turin. Some of these groups have disappeared; others still perform. But, of course, this is not really a form of theatre; it is a "tabarin"— a form unto itself, seasonal; then it's over; it doesn't take firm hold; its hold is not reproducible. I write political plays, but I have neither the desire nor the strength to fight for their performance and then, too, I am not completely confident that it is good theatre. Anyway, I think it is hard for anyone to judge his own work. And so I leave these political plays in my drawer. One of them did win a small prize. Someone stated that it was a good play, but a little heavy. So no one feels disposed to hear it out.

Q.   Will you tell us about *The Witness* — the political play
       which you both wrote and performed in?

A.   It is about the confrontation between conservative cap-
       italism and hippies. The hippy movement was just taking
       hold when I wrote the play. I think it's the only play
       that has been written on the subject of the hippies. My
       character is interesting: he doesn't know how to do any-
       thing, nor does he want to do anything. Basically, he is
       no saint. He misuses his good health in order to survive,
       and justifies himself by saying he is not interested in any-
       thing. He is just looking at the world. Then there is a
       black. My inspiration for the play was a letter written
       by a black poet to the Congress on Negritude held in
       Paris many years ago. In the letter, the poet asked his
       brothers to face the problem of choice among civiliza-
       tions in order to know which one the new third-world
       civilization should mirror. After close examination of all
       civilizations, he declared it would not be suitable to take
       a single one of them as a model, because each has given
       rise to wars, revolutions, injustices, etc. Therefore, the
       blacks must create their own civilization. So I took the
       black man as a silent witness. He never speaks a word.
       He stands motionless on the staircase landing. The idea
       came to me from the New York City blackout: a group
       of people stuck on the twenty-fifth floor of a skyscraper,
       with a radio blaring: "Don't move! Remain calm! The
       lights will go back on soon! Don't crowd the streets
       because the traffic lights are not working, and the sub-
       ways are not running. So wait patiently...". Well, the
       characters in my play waited even more patiently yet,
       and there they are discussing. Since they are all of dif-
       ferent nationalities they have different theories, and the
       black man stands there listening to their conversations
       and discussions, without ever uttering a word...a bit as
       children stand and look on. The black man is there
       looking on and does not state his impression, but it is the
       impression that we all have, which is the same as his, and
       that's the whole idea... What is strange is that even
       though this is a moderately leftist play, the Right ac-
       claimed it much more than the Left. I suppose it's be-
       cause for the Left the fact of being leftist is so logical and
       natural that it does not even permit of discussion. So the

Left said: "Bah! Foolish things! too stupid! It's like asking Adam and Eve's nationality!" For them it was too stupid. It had no sense. But for me it does. Because, in effect, we are the ones who have to look ourselves in the face. I am of the conviction that the world is ours; that it belongs to no one and to everyone. We have the possibility of tearing down these stupid barriers; we can walk, stop where we want, do what we want, just so long as we don't kill or rob or harm anyone. There is room in this world for everyone, provided we all have a little courtesy and good manners. But maybe we still have far to go before reaching the stage of courtesy. The first ones who need it, it seems to be, are those in power, because it is precisely they who lack it. The search for peace on the part of governments is an economic search and not a real search for man's well-being. No one searches for this well-being because each one is self-restrained or has preferences, which is not unhuman but is not human either. Last night I was speaking with an Algerian and I told him I was on Israel's side more than on the Arabs' side — not because I hate the Arabs but because I think it is necessary for Israel to be recognized as a nation. Only for that reason. I don't understand why someone who sides with Israel has to be a Zionist and why one who sides with the Vietcong can not be a Vietcongist. So I am a Vietcongist because I side with them. And I do so because it seems to me that they are absolutely right. A people that has been disturbed for years, first by the French and then the Americans, and which subsequently had every right to live its own way, probably would not have seen such massacre if it had been left alone. It would have done what every new nation does. Every man tries to diffuse his ideas. Perhaps they would not have done it by force. But now they have to use force.

So, in my opinion, this research for the possession of the earth, even a liberal, peaceful possession of the earth by men is not desired by anyone, because no one wants to give up his place. Today, you don't even give up your place in the trolley to a woman. Not even if she is pregnant. That's the point we have reached.

TURI FERRO

Interviewer's Note:

Turi (Salvatore) Ferro is a stage, movie, and television actor, and the Artistic Director of the Stabile Theatre of Catania (Sicily). Born in Catania on January 10, 1921, he first came to the public attention in 1950 as a young actor with the Anselmi-Abruzzo Company. Anxious to revive the Sicilian theatre according to his own lights, Ferro undertook the management of a theatrical company in 1953 together with his actress wife, Ida Carrara. They staged two Pirandello plays, *Cap and Bells* and *Sicilian Limes*, and Rosso di San Secondo's *Sleeping Beauty (La Bella Addormentata)*, but hard times followed and Ferro was obliged to spend most of his time working for the Italian radio. His very successful stage presentation in 1957 of Pirandello's *Liolà*, however, led to the formation of the *Ente Teatro di Sicilia*, which was highly acclaimed for its performances on the island, and then went to Rome with a repertory of Pirandello, Capuana and Martoglio. Turi Ferro became well-known throughout Italy as Sicily's leading actor, in the tradition of Angelo Musco, for his theatrical contributions in dialect, and for his "torrential fantasy" in portraying a variety of old, young, comic, pathetic and incoherent characters on the stage.

Q.   Your career started in the South of Italy, but now your fame has reached national proportions. Will you tell us about the development of your theatrical career?

A.   It has been like an ink-blot. I started out, in Sicily, fearful and timid, at the age of thirty-five. Then I took my Pirandello North: *Liolà, Cap and Bells* — my Pirandello. Pirandello is my author; it is he who moulded me; it is he who gave me life; it is he who allowed me to go North and spread like an ink-blot. Pirandello gave me the possibility of gaining the good will of a national

public — not through my television and movie popularity
which has recently pounced on me, so to speak—but
precisely through the theatre. I do not come from a
family of artists. My father was a professional man, but
a dilettante of note, a noteworthy theatre-lover at a time
when theatre-lovers were actors and professionals who
devoted their free time to the theatre. So, technically
speaking, I suppose I should say that I didn't learn anything from my father, but his world did become mine.
I took on his inner spirit — that is, his deep and overflowing humanity. He was everybody's Papa Ferro. I
was a nervous boy, I ran around pulling people's wagons
impertinently, I stuck moustaches on my face with bread
dough, because I didn't know that they grew, but to me
they looked real, those moustaches. Everything seemed
credible to me. Everything I have ever done, from child-
hood up to today, has always seemed credible. This is
perhaps due to the feelings I inherited from my father,
who should have become an actor. Had he done so, he
might have been a great actor today. But he had his
children and his problems to think about; his life as a
man and a father caused him to slide off in another
direction, so he never became an actor. All this enthusiasm that I put into everything I do is, perhaps, a
form of redemption for what my father did not do. The
fact that I now find myself an actor—and many would
consider that I have reached the actor's highest goal —
for me is the comfort of knowing that perhaps I haven't
even started. I feel that I still have much to give, and
much to do. So that's why I belong to the theatre.
That's why theatre will never grow old for me. And why
I don't want to stop at Verga or at Pirandello. I want to
assimilate everything that is happening in the theatre today and everything that will be happening in the future.

Q.   What are the origins of Catania's Stabile Theatre?

A.   The Stabile of Catania was born as an expression of free
       theatre — that is, a theatre that simultaneously has roots
       in tradition, is a theatre of rebirth, and a theatre of re-
       search. Our theatre is *Italian* in the sense that it is
       Mediterranean — solar theatre. In it converge the prob-
       lems that are solely and essentially problems of Italians,

but nourished and enriched by the experience of contemporary world theatre. Our theatre inherits from
Verism and Naturalism, which are, after all, the principal
resources of Italian dramaturgy, starting with Capuana,
Martoglio, Pirandello, the literary world of the human
condition of the downtrodden, and extending to Brancati, Leonardo Sciascia, and, very recently, Giuseppe
Fava, who has written about the problems of the mafia in
a play that we have taken on tour. We have, of course,
toured all of Italy, and have also gone abroad. We took
Pirandello's *Liolà* and *Cap and Bells* to South America,
and we have performed in London, Moscow, Leningrad,
Vienna, Paris, etc. The Stabile of Catania is the South-
ernmost of Italy's eight subsidized theatres. It has tried
to present a coherent message for the entire nation; that
is, we have not stopped at exclusively regional experiences, but have broadened our message through universal
plays that belong to theatre in general and to literature
in general, even though by doing so we have gone astray
from the experimental efforts of the theatre of the
South. We do understand that the Stabile Theatres,
since they enjoy State subsidies, are obliged to search
for and present certain texts, yet in order to instruct the
public and get it really to know theatre — a public that
has gradually drifted away from the theatre in search of
other experiences— we realized that it was necessary to
start from the beginning. The public has to know where
the theatre started, it has to know about Verism, etc.
Verga's *Mastro Don Gesualdo,* which we intend to put
on in a theatrical transposition by Diego Fabbri, is the
starting point of a whole Italian atmosphere that we are
reputed to have made known to a non-reading Italian
public. Our *Mastro Don Gesualdo* will be handled in
contemporary perspective and taken from the socio-
political point of view. All world theatre that uses current events as theatrical material does the same. Old
theatre, from Molière to Courteline, tells about what is
inside but also demonstrates socio-political facts. We
think we have succeeded in this respect. If things go on
as they have, that is, if more and more people drift away
from the theatre, there is still a large public that flocks
to the theatre as a popular event. The theatre is becoming more totally accepted than ever before. The danger

in Italy is that the theatre puts on lovely, new productions, but it remains a court theatre, a "club" theatre, so,
necessarily, a mafia theatre just for us — *cosa nostra*— and
we don't succeed in broadening its base. So our goal is to
move ahead, to feed more and more into the Italian
theatre so that it will expand according to the principle
that the professional conscience can be satisfied only
insofar as it absorbs as much as possible all the experiences of the international world theatre.

Q.   So is a revival of the Italian theatre in sight?

A.   There is a tendency toward a revival, but our situation is
       this: there are a lot of actors, but few people who write
       for the theatre. Many write for the comic strips; many
       write serials for magazines; and many write for the
       movies, because of this unfortunate race for money and
       easy living. Each of us has to be practical. Life is such
       today that you need a lot of money to live. Poets grad-
       ually get involved in these realities, and they must make a
       compromise. In times past, writers wrote for actors;
       today, instead, the actor has to chase after a script suited
       to his expressive forces.

Q.   How has the cinema affected dialect theatre?

A.   A certain type of cinema has distorted public taste. A
       lot of ironic movies are being made in Italy, full of am-
       biguities about the facts of life as we live them each day.
       This leads inevitably to the creating of characters which
       the contemporary public must be able to recognize; so
       the master cannot speak like his servant, who, in the
       traditional theatre, speaks with perfect diction. In the
       master-servant relationship, the latter must express him-
       self in sounds directly related to his body and his brain.
       This is the preparation — let's say the basis — required
       for the representation of the character. This bad practice
       has now reached the theatre, which has undergone the
       bad effects of a certain kind of movies. Now, if dialect
       theatre were alive at this moment in Sicily, or if we de-
       cided to have a Venetian theatre, a Milanese theatre, a
       Sicilian theatre, or a Neapolitan theatre, I think it would
       be hugely successful — but on the popular level. That is,

I think that Molière, writing in his language, would not
have the actors playing the parts of certain characters,
masks, silly servants, cooks, etc. — those actors who in
his time were actor-authors, concerned about preserving
linguistic preciseness — would not have those actors
speak the official language. They would use dialect. We
get this with Strehler, too, sometimes. Strehler today
has attracted world attention. In his dialect presentations — *Our Milan (El Nost Milan)* and *Quarrels in Chiog-
gia (Le Baruffe Chiozzotte)*— he poses theatre precisely
as language, that is, he wants to establish the existence of
dialect by rendering it noble. Naturally, some dialects
are better equipped than others. The Venetian theatre
is more lively; it has scripts, and Venice is one of the
regions of Italy that has the mask tradition: Punch,
Harlequin, Pantaloon, etc. The Sicilian theatre doesn't
have this, but we have a special world. They say we are a
happy people; that we are a sulky people, that we are a
frustrated people with problems. So maybe our theatre
makes up for the lack of masks by presenting a grotesque
human condition, reflected today in the modern theatre.

Q.   Shakespeare and Pirandello are both very modern in this
respect, aren't they?

A.   When we speak of modern theatre, Shakespeare is really
the greatest— that is, he is the most modern. Pirandello
stirred up the feeling of the insanity of life as seen
through the projected prism of men's weaknesses, follies,
solitude and arrogance. Pirandello points these things
out. His is a theatre of reproach. Shakespeare has
shown all these things in his tragedies and comedies: the
good, the bad, the courageous, the beautiful, the ugly.
The force of his plays is such that even today, if our
contemporaries want to reach their height or want to
create theatre anew, it suffices to take a Shakespeare
play, and it will give you the most modern production
in existence today.

A.   Is there any connection between the Greek theatre,
which is frequently performed in Sicily in the ancient
amphitheatres, and the contemporary Sicilian theatre?

A.   We have, perhaps, taken from the Greeks more than
       their civilization and their classical essentiality. We
       have inherited our way of expressing ourselves from the
       Greek language, and we have taken from the Greek
       theatre all its asperity. For example, when Sicilians say:
       "Watch out when you cross the street!", it is like a tragic
       outcry. This is because the Greek theatre imagines it-
       self as an entrusted force of the gods. In addition, be-
       cause of the various foreign conquests of Sicily, our
       theatre is highly eclectic: we have been under Spanish
       domination, so there is something of Garcia Lorca in us;
       we are Norman and French; there is a certain German ex-
       pressionism in us. Remember that Pirandello studied in
       Bonn. So we have been struggling to find our own
       identity... And we express our suffering with irony.
       Undoubtedly world theatre and Greek theatre have
       greatly influenced Southern theatre, the Sicilian theatre,
       and, therefore, the Italian theatre.

Q.   Does Catania, as a center and as the seat of the Stabile
       Theatre, serve other theatres in the region as well?

A.   Yes. We perform in many regional theatres. This is why
       I said before that although the theatre seemed to be
       losing out to other media, now it is regaining its place,
       partly because it is becoming popular. Before, these
       theatres in the region had served as movie-houses. Ours
       is one of the few cases in the Italian theatre where, in-
       stead of a theatre occupying a former movie-house, a
       movie-house re-became a theatre. We have very few
       theatres in Sicily, but they are sufficient to contain quite
       a large public. And here in Sicily we can see the public's
       desire to converge in theatres more than in any other
       place of cultural entertainment, and its willingness to
       travel thirty or forty or one hundred kilometers in order
       to see one of our performances.

Q.   What do you think of the foreign public that comes to
       see performances in Sicily?

A.   Well, there are all kinds of audiences. We don't consider
       tourists a qualified public. In general, we have to choose
       our theatre-going public, and it wouldn't be the tourists

who come to Sicily to attend a certain type of performance. Exception must be made here of the Greek theatre of Syracuse (Siracusa), and the Greek theatre of Taormina which, in reality, are Italian theatre, "peninsula" theatre, as we say. The fact is that the tourist wants theatre that casts him into the local color and folklore of Sicily, to see all the novelties that help him to get to know the place he is visiting better.

Q. How would you characterize the local Sicilian public?

A. It isn't that the Sicilian public is not prepared and not intelligent. I believe that in order to approach the theatre, you need more than preparation. You need sensitivity, and the public is sensitive to everything. But perhaps we have been too much in conflict. We have had the war, and there was a sharp cut-off— that is, we began where others left off. Others had discovered everything before us. We, in order to catch up, had to take long strides and perhaps they were longer than they should have been. So our public is disoriented, but there is a big difference between today's public and that of 1959. Today, innovation, contemporaneity and modernity are accepted, whereas a decade ago they were not. So we have had the opportunity of rendering our public a responsible one, which is responding to the revival in the theatre. Of course there is still a part of the public that feels theatre to be a form of popular amusement, but there are more people interested in reviving the theatre than those seeking amusement.

Q. What difference do you see between young audiences and old ones?

A. The young are more "available," more disposed to getting the message. The old are beginning to understand, however, through young people, that they, too, have to be revived.

Q. What does the Stabile Theatre of Catania do to attract young people to the theatre?

A. We have theatre for the schools. We have a school for

performances for young people who may even be included in our casts each year. In addition, we have an experimental theatre for reading or performing extracts of modern authors. We have a director on the spot. We have a committee to read texts — a sort of research laboratory through which contacts with the young are established. And we give special performances on Thursdays and Saturdays for young people. Then the plays are repeated, with young people of the secondary and high schools and other institutions playing the roles. We really attract the public, and our policy is to make the ticket prices attractive too: 350 lire (about sixty cents). So we provide theatre for students, but naturally we don't invade their classrooms. We do have meetings, technical discussions and conferences with them in the classrooms, treating all sorts of theatrical subjects, and we try to draw from them their reactions to the plays they have seen, and get them to express what they have derived from their theatrical experiences.

Q.   What is the reaction of non-Sicilians to your Sicilian theatre?

A.   Well, I'm not really the one who should answer this question but if I may speak personally and subjectively, my inner world is not a world of words or of particular modes of expression; it is rather a world of gesture. Gesture is innate in me. Therefore, sometimes an image created by a gesture, a movement, a tempo, can express more than an author may have foreseen — even if the author is Pirandello. Pirandello is great in that he put himself into the shoes of the actor who could have expressed concepts even before uttering the words. Sometimes, when I find myself before an audience in Trieste or Milan, I find I am using more words for that particular public. It may even happen that in Sicily I have to use more words. But in Moscow, and Leningrad, many lines that the Italians didn't catch were understood by the Soviet public, which undoubtedly understands that unique feeling in the theatre: the moment of exteriorization of the actor's feeling. Or maybe the public there is more qualified, or has a more developed theatrical attitude, or is better prepared because it frequents the theatre more.

Q.   Has the Soviet public received preparation for the Italian
       theatre, and especially for the dialect theatre?

A.   I don't think so. I have met Soviet actors who have per-
       formed in Pirandello. They find his plays to contain
       great naturalistic strength. We in Italy are still tied to
       Stanislawski, while the Soviets have already moved away
       from him. They see us as still marking time. They say
       we perform the way the Bulgarians and the Romanians
       do; that our performances resemble those in the South
       of the Eastern European countries. But they undoubt-
       edly find in the Italian theatre a power and captivation
       which they appreciate, and which is lacking in their own
       theatre.

Q.   What do you think of Brecht?

A.   Brecht is certainly the latest monster in the contempor-
       ary theatre. First we had Menander, then Shakespeare,
       Chekhov, Pirandello, Molière, etc. and now we have
       Brecht. There is no problem in getting the public to
       listen to him. Absolutely not! I think we will wait a
       long time before we have another form of theatre. At
       least fifty years will have to elapse.

Q.   Do you prefer the conventional stage or an open-air
       theatre?

A.   I think in terms of the closed theatre only, because
       theatre is an act of love that can be made only in privacy.
       I consider the open-air theatre a popular genre, a theatre
       of movement, a threatre that drags you along, a theatre
       that dazzles. My sort of theatre is intimate, so it is
       necessarily indoor theatre. I don't think I could com-
       municate my inner drama to such a vast audience.

Q.   Should plays, then, continue to be given in traditional
       style? Are footlights, velvet curtain, and loges necessary?

A.   Absolutely not! A theatre of inner emotion does not
       imply these things. In fact, many of my fellow actors

regret the days when spectators sat on the stage, where they really could see the actors' eyes. It's true. The eyes are the mirror of the exchange between actor and public, and the public doesn't even get to see the eyes. However, today we have total theatre, and it's no longer a question of the ham actor coming out on stage to show off. I think you can have theatre in the box-office: you can put the actors in the box-office and the audience on stage rather than in the middle of the hall. You can put the audience on the platform, or vice versa. In sum, it's a question of establishing a theatrical tradition that creates emotion. So red velvet and gold, false splendor and tinsel, are things that age the theatre, even from the psychological point of view.

Q.   What was your reaction to the Living Theatre?

A.   Like all forms of theatre of provocation, the Living Theatre naturally disconcerted the public at first. But then some people assumed the responsibility of understanding and accepting this experimental force. Others, instead, rejected it completely. I, personally, am in favor of all new forces. I, too, am searching, would like to move ahead, and accept anything that is capable of arousing my emotions. The Living Theatre did move me; it made me think; and, therefore, it was useful in the sense that one can extract from the experience things to put into other experiences that are structured more as poetic reality. I love a poetic reality—even though it be madness—ot the human condition but one that does not take me too far away from reality, because then the act of love, and the colloquium become dishumanized; they become rarified; and they lose that amount of concrete relationship that is required in everything.

Q.   Do you think that because of the serious financial problems facing it, the theatre in Italy will die?

A.   Your question justifies what I said earlier: that today, the actor, the writer, the technician, are drifting away, in part, toward those media that are more rewarding financially. There is no doubt, however, that the living force that the theatre is will never be lost, because theatre is created, and will have to be created, and has always been created, since the beginning, by people who are not pre-occupied with money. This is why the theatre can never die.

LUIGI DE FILIPPO

Interviewer's Note:

Luigi De Filippo is a member of the famous De Filippo family of Neapolitan actors and authors in dialect and in Italian. Son of Peppino and actress Adele Carloni, Luigi has been acting for eighteen years in his father's company, which was formed in 1945 after the two brothers, Peppino and Eduardo, broke apart.
    Luigi De Filippo is also the author of two plays: *Our Business* and *Strange Story on a Roman Terrace.*

Q.   How long have you been in the threatre?

A.   I have been performing for the past eighteen years, and three years ago I began writing plays because I felt the need—more than a vocation— the need to write plays suitable for myself. Two of them have been very successful.

Q.   Do you mind my asking about any possible father-son rivalry?

A.   Naturally, having to make a place for oneself between two giants of the theatre like Eduardo and Peppino is not easy. But I try not to think about it, to go straight ahead on my own path. Besides, I am aware that the public is encouraging me in what I am doing by showing me much affection and esteem. So I try to maintain an autonomous style and humor, completely different from Eduardo's and Peppino's style.

Q.   Will you tell us something about the contemporary Neapolitan theatre?

A.   Eduardo, whose latest plays you are familiar with, writes for the Neapolitan theatre; my father, Peppino De

Filippo, writes in Italian; he hasn't been writing in dialect for many years now. Then there are younger authors, like myself. As I mentioned earlier, I have written two plays, which were very successful here in Italy: *Our Business (Fatti Nostri)* and *Strange Story on a Roman Terrace (Storia Strana su di una terrazza romana)*, which I took to Rome, Milan, Naples, Bari, Turin, and Genova — most of the principal theatres, in sum, and also to Trieste.

Q. The De Filippo family, besides being actors, are also playwrights, which places you in a different theatrical tradition. What are the origins of this tradition? Have you created your own school?

A. Well, we try to remain in the tradition of the *commedia dell'arte*, but naturally without wearing masks on stage since they are out of style. We want to continue the traditions of the Italian comedy of the sixteenth century by bringing to the stage today's personages, today's characters, contemporary problems — all that can interest today's public. Theatre as conceived by my father, by me, by Eduardo in dialect, is the bringing to the stage of contemporary society, but in the style, presentation and characterization that derive from the *commedia dell'arte*. We have created — at least Eduardo and Peppino have, long before me — a *genre* which in turn has created a certain type of school. So many Italian actors today are products of that school. They began with Eduardo and Peppino, and then gradually went out on their own, creating their own personalities and making their name in other theatrical companies, but the matrix and the roots are there.

Q. The De Filippo theatre, then, cannot be considered dialect theatre?

A. No; I would say no, that it is not limited to dialect theatre inasmuch as we try to bring to the stage a mirror of the Italian realities of today, that it is not solely a retrospective theatre, nor a solely academic theatre, but rather a living, current theatre that concerns today's audiences.

Q.   Your plays, then, are understood and appreciated in all
      the regions of Italy. And I believe you have also toured
      abroad?

A.   Yes, I have toured abroad with my father. We have per-
      formed in Paris, London, Warsaw, Moscow and Prague.

Q.   Not in the United States?

A.   Neither Eduardo, Peppino nor I have ever performed in
      the United States. One of Eduardo's plays —*Filomena
      Marturano,* I think — has been performed in the United
      States. Peppino and I have been to South America.

Q.   What was your experience in Moscow? How were you
      received there?

A.   We were in Moscow five years ago, and we toured for two
      and a half months: Moscow, Leningrad, and many other
      Soviet cities. The public we met was really sophisticated,
      theatre-wise. They were devoted to the theatre, and es-
      pecially to the Italian theatre, which they love. The en-
      thusiasm of those young people who flocked to the the-
      atres was really an extraordinary thing. We offered them
      one of my father's plays, *The Metamorphoses of a
      Travelling Musician (Le Metamorfosi di un suonatore
      ambulante)* and Machiavelli's *The Mandrake.*

Q.   Which audience in Italy best appreciates and understands
      you?

A.   I don't think one can be selective and say that the North
      likes us or the South likes us. Our theatre is generally
      appreciated by both North and South. No cities like us
      more than others. I would say that we are received well
      everywhere—because, as I said before, our theatre mir-
      rors today's society.

Q.   How does the theatre in Northern Italy differ from that
      of the South?

A.   The answer is a bit complex. In the North — the indus-
      trial triangle of Italy — the theatre is mainly financed by

the State, so naturally the repertory is essentially political, so to speak. Since it is subsidized by the government, which is Center-Left, a particular type of theatre is actually being subsidized: principally authors like Brecht — leftists, principally. But Brecht appeals to a small part only of the general public. The general audience — the audience that is accustomed to paying the regular price of a ticket — prefers another type of theatre. Our repertory, for example.

The theatre of the North doesn't have financial problems inasmuch as it is subsidized by the State. So they don't care whether the public attends or not. They have a political stance vis-à-vis the public, regardless of whether the public comes to their theatres or not. A private theatrical company, on the other hand, with its own capital, and not dependent on the State — as Peppino's or Eduardo's— offers a somewhat different theatre. Theirs is not essentially political. Theirs is theatre for the sake of theatre. The objective of their theatre is to entertain a public interested in intelligent, contemporary matters — not in a political discourse. The State-subsidized theatre can offer tickets at a very low price. The best seats sell for very little, in order to help certain working classes. A private company, such as Eduardo's or Peppino's, cannot do this.

Q. Besides the famous De Filippo plays, do you keep renewing your repertory?

A. Yes, of course! Eduardo doesn't, however. He performs only his own plays. Peppino's repertory is vaster than Eduardo's. Peppino and I have done Molière, Macchiavelli, Plautus, Pirandello, and many, many other authors, both Italian and foreign.

Q. Do you modify and adapt these texts, or do you leave them in their original form?

A. They are left as they were written, although we naturally try to give them a modern interpretation without, however, altering the spirit of the work.

Q. Do you think the type of theatre created by the De

Filippo family will disappear after they are gone? ·

A.   No, I don't think so. And I say this based on my ex-
       perience of what happens in the theatre: every hundred
       years or so the phenomenon of the actor-author re-
       appears. He presents and performs in plays written by
       himself. It is generally said that after this actor-author
       dies, his plays will die with him. It doesn't work that
       way, however. After a certain period of time − seventy
       or eighty years − an actor appears on the scene who has
       the capacity of reviving those plays and presenting them
       in his own interpretation, his own style, which differ
       from those of his predecessors. What I mean is that our
       repertory will not end with us; it will always −after
       many years−find an interpreter who will recognize the
       theatrical validity of our plays and who will perform
       them according to his own sensitivities and his own
       artistic possibilities. This always happens in the theatre.

Q.   What is the Neapolitan attitude toward theatre today?

A.   In the last two or three years, here in Naples, there has
       been greatly renewed interest in the theatre on the part
       of the public. Up to three or four years ago, Naples was
       not a theatre-going city for so many reasons: social,
       economic, because of television that drew the public
       away from the theatres, etc. Now, however, in the last
       two or three years, the public has been drawn consider-
       ably closer to the theatre. And Naples has become a very
       "theatrical" city − just as it was thirty years ago.

Q.   Is the revival of interest in the theatre more marked
       among the young or the old?

A.   I feel it's among young people. That's strange, don't you
       think? In this age of polemic that we are living through,
       young people love to go back to the theatre to see the
       old comedies, which take on an active flavor for them.
       They love to see what they've heard their parents talk
       about. We tell these young people wonderful things,
       which they cannot forget. It's true. Maybe they've
       understood this. They are re-discovering meaningful
       things which they understand must not be discarded;

things that must be loved, learned, known and preserved because they are every man's patrimony. These wonderful things inspire beautiful sentiments when they are heard—even today.

Q.   How does the Neapolitan public react to foreign theatre? To the theatre of the absurd? To a Ionesco?

A.   I would say that it accepts foreign theatre more through snobbishness than through conviction. It really shows no marked preference for foreign theatre. No, I don't think a theatre of the absurd could last long in Naples, and I think the facts bear me out. Naples is perhaps more bound to traditional theatre; it prefers it; it loves it more. It isn't very receptive to these experiments that come from abroad or the innovations that come from Rome or Milan which are, theatrically speaking, more open cities.

Q.   What has the future in store for you?

A.   I have just finished writing a play on a very live subject: the problem that afflicts Rome, and Italy in general, because they are over-loved by tourists. The whole Italian historic patrimony is falling into ruin, and the State is not giving enough attention to the problem. Monuments and museums are crumbling within the nation, and no one realizes it. I don't know whether you have read the newspaper reports on the decay of the Coliseum and the Arch of Titus. Well, I have written a satirical comedy on the subject. I hope to present it in Rome, next April.

Q.   Do radio, television and cinema take up much of your time?

A.   The movies, much less than before. For the last three or four years, it's the theatre that has been occupying us mainly, especially with our foreign tours. Radio and television occupy us more than the cinema.

CHECCO DURANTE [1]

Interviewer's Note:

The late Checco Durante was a stage, movie and radio actor, and Rome's best-known contemporary dialect dramatic author and poet. He was born in the Trastevere section of Rome on November 19, 1893. He began in the theatre as an amateur, but a chance meeting with Ettore Petrolini, the famous Roman comic actor, convinced Durante that he should devote himself seriously to the stage. After an association with Petrolini that lasted from 1920 to 1928, Durante left the Petrolini Company and tried to establish a Stabile Theatre in Rome, but without success. He formed his own Company in 1933 with his actress wife Anita, born in Rome on September 28, 1897. In 1950, the Durantes made the Teatro Rossini, near the Pantheon, their permanent theatre, where they have staged Roman dialect comedies as well as comedies adapted from other dialects, especially Florentine.

The year 1973 marked the Durantes' twenty-third winter season at the Rossini, their twentieth summer season on the outdoor stage of Villa Aldobrandini in Rome, and the forty-first year of Checco's directorship of his faithful troupe which comprises, among others, his daughter Leila Ducci and his son-in-law, actor and writer Enzo Liberti.

Q.   Your troupe has been attracting audiences for the past forty-four years. Will you trace your long career?

A.   I started my career with the world-famous actor Ettore Petrolini, who started his own career in variety shows. During the first World War, he formed his theatrical troupe which travelled all over Italy. I joined them in 1918. We toured Italy and South America. I collaborated with him not only on the stage but also in writing plays. After about ten years with Petrolini, with my family growing and my finances shrinking, I was forced to go out on my own. The first few years were extremely difficult, but I finally had my breakthrough in the variety shows performed on movie-house stages. I really had my scruples about getting up there with the comedians and dancers; but my popularity grew throughout Italy. I was called to the big theatres in Naples, Palermo, Milan, Venice, Bologna. But I've never had a business mind. My theatre doesn't have commercial qualities. My public is a public that appreciates my artistic talent, and not the public that goes to the theatre to be snobbish. I've never been financially successful, but I'm happy and satisfied because I see that the public has remained faithful to me throughout the years and I'm still making a decent living. I've really never cared about financial success. One of my greatest rewards was the fact that my theatrical troupe was the first to be invited to perform for Italians on African stages during the African wars. I returned to Italy just at the start of World War II, to the Quattro Fontane Theatre in Rome. But then I was asked to perform for our soldiers stationed throughout Italy. I didn't question whether the war was right or wrong. I guess in my own mind I thought it was wrong. Anyway, thousands of Italian soldiers were waiting for me to perform for them. My shows were a great success, and I'm proud of them even today. I still receive letters and donations from some of the soldiers, from all over Italy. It's interesting that even though I couldn't understand their various dialects— Sicilian, Milanese, Venetian, etc.—*they* understood and enjoyed my Roman slang and jokes. They added a tone of Italian universality to my Roman dialect performances.

Q.   Will you explain the characteristics of your Roman dialect theatre?

A.   My theatre was born of my great love for the city of Rome. I was born in one of the poorest sections of Rome: Trastevere. As a boy, my great desire was to give the city a theatre of its own. Often, when a local theatre is created, the worst aspects of the region are stressed and the inhabitants wind up having a false and exagger-

ated reputation. Romans had often been represented on
the stage as showoffs and do-nothings—in order to attract
the public. But they absolutely do not have these characteristics. I've known them for over seventy years. I
know that the typical Roman is, perhaps, a bit lazy, a
chronic complainer, and quickly aroused if a wrong is
done him, but basically he is good, kindhearted, humane,
expansive, faithful in friendship, attached to his family
and to his work, and a good sport. So I wanted to create
a popular theatre that would reflect all the best qualities
of the Romans, and still be authentic.

Q.   What was your attitude during Italy's period of fascism?

A.   I have never in my life played politics—first, because I've
never understood politics and, second, because I believe
that art stands above any political involvement. In any
case, to answer your question, I managed to stay out and
live my own life. Fascism—after an initial period of tur-
bulence—became a stable way of life in Italy. Because I
have always believed that what counts in life is sincerity,
honesty and simplicity, I have made these my life-style
and have never gotten into any trouble. But I've never
been afraid to bring to the stage any humoristic political
criticism that might afford entertainment for the public.

Q.   Is your dialect theatre comparable to that of the De
Filippos in Naples? Are there differences among the
various dialect actors?

A.   The De Filippos' genre and mine are both dialect theatres. But the De Filippo brothers, especially Eduardo,
has detached himself from dialect theatre. He has not remained faithful to the tradition but rather has slowly
evolved toward a modern, contemporary theatre, in
which the character assumes a specific personality. My
theatre, instead, has remained one hundred per cent
dialect. Its subject matter is not fixed or prearranged. I
bring to the stage the everyday life of the common
people—and there is no hidden meaning. I can interpret
without difficulty *any* situation; I can impersonate *any*
character, without studying the role. I enter into the
personage and live out his life. I believe that the *sim-*

plicity of these performances, stressing the most natural and most touching experiences, affords the spectator a sentimental diversion. But this type of art is more acceptable to the general public than to the critics.

There are differences among the various dialect actors, even though they all try to bring out the characteristic features of the people in their region. Some of the actors have allowed themselves to change in order to become more universally accepted. In some cases, the change has been profitable, financially speaking. Instead, my type of performance has remained unchanged all through the years, and I suppose this is the reason for my poor financial standing.

Q. It seems that the Italian theatre in general, and the dialect theatre in particular, has been going through a critical period over the past decade. Is there now a renewed interest in the theatre, as some media would indicate?

A. It's true that there has been a crisis in the theatrical world, but the dialect theatre will live as long as the dialect actor lives, and it will die with the actor. As a matter of fact, once the actor dies in a particular region, that region no longer has a theatre. Rome had no dialect theatre before us. Now, it's possible to adopt the concepts of our theatre to other regions and cities, but those concepts have to be transformed to suit the mentality of a particular audience. All of this depends on the ability of the actor to assimilate regional characteristics and to bring to the local public versions of their own life-style.

Q. What will happen to the Roman dialect theatre after you are gone?

A. Perhaps there will be some one to carry on. I think, however, that the performances will be more modernized —perhaps through radio or television—and written by professionals, which means it will not be the *natural* theatre that we cherish. I think the general public will feel cheated and confused, and have trouble interpreting the meaning of these modernized performances. Perhaps a type of dialect theatre will develop in which the spectator simply will not see himself living in the part any more.

Q.   In an interview published in *Il Tempo* (a Rome daily
        newspaper), you stated that you did not want your
        niece to join the theatrical world, in view of what it has
        become. Will you explain your statement?

A.   I believe that the theatrical world has undergone a
        drastic change, not only in Italy, but all over the world.
        Everything now is based on publicity and less and less
        importance is given to the artist's talent and simplicity.
        Reputation is acquired not on the basis of an actor's
        capacity to perform but rather on the number of times
        he has changed wives and the scandals he's been involved
        in. These bits of news spread and create fame. I should
        like to see people in the theatrical world enjoy a differ-
        ent kind of success—the kind given by a public that ac-
        cepts the actor, applauds his performances, and follows
        him wherever he goes.

Q.   Are there any contemporary Italian dramatists that you
        consider great?

A.   No. I don't think any are great because, with the ten-
        dency to keep pace with the modern trend, they have
        distorted the real significance of the Italian theatre. In
        the past, Italian plays (D'Annunzio's theatre, e.g.) could
        be staged all over the world. Today, there is a tendency
        to change, transform and readapt the true Italian theatre,
        thereby spoiling or destroying it, as far as I can see.

[1] Reprinted with permission from *Drama & Theatre*, State University College, Fredonia, N.Y. (Henry F. Salerno, Ed.), Vol. II,
No. 2, Winter 1972-73.

GIORGIO ALBERTAZZI

Interviewer's Note:

Giorgio Albertazzi is a stage, screen and television actor and author, and a threatrical director as well. Born on August 20, 1926 in Fiesole (Florence), he first studied architecture, then began his dramatic career giving his first public performance in Shakespeare's *Troilus and Cressida,* directed by Luchino Visconti. He joined the Stabile Theatre of Florence in 1951, and made his first film, but he feels there is an incompatibility between himself and cinema. In 1955 he organized a theatrical group which he took on tour to South America. The Proclemer-Albertazzi Company, subsequently formed in 1956-57, was highly acclaimed by the Italian public and performed in numerous cities at home and abroad. Its repertory at first consisted mainly of unpublished contemporary texts with a balance between foreign and Italian authors, but gradually Albertazzi tended more toward critical interpretations of the classics. From 1952 to 1959, he worked actively in television, and during 1960-61, the movies absorbed him extensively (especially his role in *Last Year at Marienbad,* 1961). He nevertheless found time to direct Diego Fabbri's version of Mauriac's *Thérèse Desqueyroux* for the stage and, during 1962 and 1963 to act for the stage in François Billetdoux's *Then Go to Törpe's* and in Franco Brusati's *The Fastidious One.* Albertazzi's 1963 performance of *Hamlet,* directed by Franco Zeffirelli, won the first prize at the Festival of Nations in Paris, and subsequently was seen in Zurich, Vienna, and at the Old Vic in London.

Albertazzi alternates between television and theatre, the two activities forming a sort of ensemble. He is one of the most representative figures among Italy's post-war actors: cultured, modern, and convinced of the esthetic, moral and civil functions of the theatre.

Q.   What are the highlights in your twenty-year long career?

A.   Since I am such an "available" person, people do with me
        what they will. I am at everyone's disposal. Anybody at
        all can occupy my time — during the day, the night, and
        even during my working hours. So I end up doing the
        things that others want me to do and rarely do I do the
        things *I* want to do. But I don't regret it, because what-
        ever I do I do with love, either for a person or a group.
        Well, the things I really wanted to do can be counted on
        one hand. They are: my television performance in
        Dostoyevsky's *The Idiot,* for which I also wrote the
        script, and Stevenson's *Dr. Jekyll and Mr. Hyde,* which I
        prepared for Italian television and which I directed and
        performed in. I gave it a new twist by transposing the
        elements of Stevenson's thriller — which is much more
        than a dective story, of course. I made the protagonist a
        molecular biologist who is working on the brain in order
        to study hereditary factors in DNA. By transmitting
        messages through his double, he succeeds in changing his
        own cerebral structure and therefore in transforming him-
        self into a being that is always — and this is the impor-
        tance of the text — the other being that is inside us. We
        are never *one;* there is always the dark brother, as Ameri-
        can biologists say, and that is the natural man. Not the
        pure savage, which we no longer are, but instinctive man.
        This was Jekyll. The television play was very successful
        in Italy; it was sold to foreign countries; but it was a
        black-and-white production, so neither the United States
        nor England bought it. It competed for the 1972 prize in
        Italy, but unfortunately it was in black and white! That's
        the point. So I have talked about two of my television
        productions. The others, which I did just to please
        others, I shall not mention. As for the theatre, the first
        play I directed was Sartre's *The Condemned of Altona,*
        which I also produced and performed in. My first efforts
        at directing went very well, but as soon as I began doing
        what others told me to do, the results were less good.
        I'll mention also my two interpretations of *Hamlet:* one
        summer production directed by a young Cambridge di-
        rector, and the second by Franco Zeffirelli, which we
        took to the Paris Festival of Nations, where it won in the
        competition. We then took it to London, in 1964, at
        Sir Laurence Olivier's invitation, where I played Hamlet
        twenty-five times during the Shakespeare centenary. We

also took it to Vienna, etc. I've only mentioned two highlights in my theatrical career, and I'll talk about just one more: *Pilate Forever,* which I wrote in 1972 and which is the first complete text written by me. It was performed during the 1972-73 season in Italy, and then we took it to South America. In this play, too, there is a transposition of the myth of the contemporary political manager. There is a sort of see-sawing between Pilate's historic position and today's situation: we are all Pilates. This is the theme of my play. It's a serious and important one, for in Italy today, the political climate is regressive, democracy is far from being liberal, and all political forces are struggling for power rather than for the emancipation of man. A text like *Pilate Forever* is very disturbing because it doesn't satisfy anyone in the political spectrum. Certain extra-parliamentarians might have given it their support, but perhaps they had other things to do, or perhaps there are too few of them. In any case, my play was not popular — that is, it was directed toward only a few. It is the first play of anarchical inspiration that has been performed in Italy. I believe that *Pilate Forever* constitutes a new type of dramaturgy— a dramaturgy of the future. I don't say it's the first and only play of its kind, but the idea is this: we no longer want written, untouchable texts from which the author remains absent. We want theatre to be an idea of theatre, at which we can all work to achieve a certain result — the result of liberation and communication, in which the public can participate. I think this is pretty much what is happening—not only here in Italy. A closed text, a script to be interpreted willy-nilly, no longer interests us. It seems anachronistic and useless. Maybe it's because there are no more geniuses around. If Shakespeare or Molière should return to this earth, naturally we would say: "Fine!" But we must face the fact that geniuses are lacking, that actors, producers and men of the theatre need more and more to express themselves completely in their work. Express themselves means to participate in the theatrical act with their very life, their own opinions, their own political ideas. Not just like a mechanism of artificial technical expression.

Q.   A little like the actors of the *commedia dell'arte?*

A.   Yes, the *commedia dell'arte* comes immediately to mind.
      That's right, from one point of view. But beware! The
      commedia dell'arte in reality followed very precise
      schemata. Improvisations followed the lines of a series
      of *lazzi,* which were recited well or not so well, with a
      certain degree of inventiveness, but all of this did not in-
      volve the actor from the personal, human point of view.
      It was more a question of his bravura and his talent. I
      don't think there has been any theorizing yet about the
      kind of theatre I'm talking about, although there has been
      a series of attempts. Once, in New York, the Living
      Theatre started out giving a lecture and gradually the lec-
      ture evolved into a theatrical act. This, in my opinion, is
      theatre. No one should be aware of what is happening
      in its final terms. Then the theatrical act becomes total
      involvement. When we performed *Pilate Forever* in
      South America, we discovered that it had become polit-
      ical theatre, because the situation there was such that
      the public identified—either with the haves or the have-
      nots. In Montevideo, for example, some young men
      in the balcony began shouting: *"Queremos libertad!"*
      At that very moment, with a feeling of exciting fear,
      I made the discovery that theatre is something other
      than what we were performing. Theatre is much broad-
      er. It is a collective cement that can be made to ex-
      plode if we are all involved and all concerned; and we
      must all participate in it. Otherwise, where lies the
      strength of the theatre as contrasted with packaged
      works such as the movies? The spectator watching a
      film cannot do anything about it; the reel turns; he
      can walk out, but he cannot change what is happen-
      ing in any way whatsoever. True, authentic theatre
      is a utopian theatre. I believe only in utopias. The
      spectator at the theatre can change a performance at
      any moment he chooses. He can say: "Stop! That's
      enough!" And that's just what I am striving for.

Q.   You have acted on the stage as well as for movies and
      television. What are the differences among the three
      media from the point of view of the actor?

A.   From the actor's point of view they are three substantially different ways of expressing the same thing. In the theatre, the actor is much more of an author than in the cinema, where the author is the director and no one else. Even if the actor can intervene in some way, at the script stage or when the filming is going on, everything is still completely in the hands of the director. Television is halfway between the other two media. But which television are we talking about? Television that produces theatre? That's the most mediocre type of theatre that one can imagine. Good television has to give you the immediacy of events in direct discourse. It has to be improvised—contrary to the way it's done in Italy, where television was much more interesting ten years ago. Today, besides the fact that you can't even work for television any more because union demands (of which my friends are so proud of) are all detrimental to the final product, television has become a matter of technology. Every little interview is first taped, because of political concerns. So where is that wonderful, spontaneous, haphazard, adventurous improvisation which is the fundamental characteristic of television? In South America, where of course the level differs for cultural reasons, television is like ours ten years ago. I found values there that we have lost completely. There is one show in Buenos Aires: an actress invites to lunch five or six personalities who happen to be in town — a theatre director, a fashion designer, a painter, etc. I went, without any rehearsal. We really ate, and we conversed. That is television. When, instead, you start rehearsing, cutting, splicing, etc., then you really have to say very important things, because otherwise it's all very mediocre. In movies, you have what is called the "film specific," which is that mysterious, secret *something* — a sequence rhythm, the breathing time of cinematographic sequences. A "television specific" has not yet been found. I experienced this at the 1972 competition, with my *Dr. Jekyll and Mr. Hyde,* and I have seen it in all the television shows that are most representative of different countries: they all seem to be unsuccessful movie films. They don't have that immediacy, that impact, which television alone can have because it is the most powerful medium that exists. When I think of the times in which we are living, it is television above all that amazes me.

Looking at sports on television is the most beautiful thing in the world, because we can see the games through machines! And it's so marvelous when the machine is moved away at certain moments because they don't want you to see something! It's spectacular!

Q.   How does the Italian public react to your work? Is there a difference between the way the South and the North reacts?

A.   There are two public reactions: that of the young, and that of the traditional public. The latter thinks I have betrayed them completely. One example will suffice: during the 1972 season, I staged a work by Gabriele D'Annunzio. Now, D'Annunzio has influenced every aspect of Italian and European art since the beginning of this century. He is a great decadent and mystifier, whose theatrical works are today unstageable (with the exception of *The Daughter of Iorio*). I took one of his works — *La Gioconda* — and transformed its language; in a certain sense, I rewrote D'Annunzio's language. The public, which is profoundly ignorant, didn't realize what I had done and it so happened that the play was acceptable. Why? Because Italians are D'Annunzian, in spite of everything. That is, D'Annunzio is inside of them: conquest of women, curtain of mystery, mixture of sacred and profane, profanation, beautiful words, sharp challenges. Actually, none of this is true. It's all *pro forma.* At any rate, at the Manzoni Theatre in Milan, for example, "*La Gioconda* di D'Annunzio" brought in two and a half million lire daily (abour $4,000)! The public was buying seats ten days in advance! You would have thought it was New York! Some of the critics — the politically involved ones, shall we say —turned on me. They didn't understand that it was a profoundly political act to perform D'Annunzio in that way. They didn't understand. But critics scarcely ever understand. The following year, 1973, at the same theatre, at the same time of year, I put on *Pilate Forever.* Not even a million lire a day (about $1,600)! Not even an average of a million lire came in. Not even half of the *La Gioconda* receipts. On opening night, I could sense that the good people of Milan were stiff with surprise and indignation.

They said: "How is it possible? We've lost even Albertazzi! Who knows what bad company has influenced him! He has betrayed us. We were accustomed to his restless talent, but we never expected him to go over to the other side! He is talking against us!" Yes, I was talking against them, because that's just what I wanted to do. And so it was perhaps only because our Company — Anna Proclemer's and mine, had such a solid reputation, that the theatre wasn't empty. Italians, especially in the industrial cities of the North—Milan and Turin—turned thumbs down on *Pilate Forever*, while the Southern cities, which are less culturalized in the technological sense, which are unhappier and therefore more disposed to reflections on man, accepted the play. Youth accepted it, because they found it contained a message of concern to them. The argument contained in *Pilate Forever* is often discussed among young people, or if it is not discussed openly, it is at least felt by all of them.

Underlying all of this, there is a conception of the theatre: traditionally, people go to the theatre in Paris, in Rome, in Milan, in New York, to be entertained and amused — even to become absorbed— but never to go to bed. Theatre, however, means just that: go to bed with someone, and I don't mean go to bed to talk! Theatre is copulative, or it's nothing. Theatre is not an appointment with someone in a café, nor is it a pleasant conversation on the theme of love. Theatre is making love. Definitely.

Q. Does your interpretation of a role change as you rehearse?

A. I change my interpretations continuously — every evening — according to my mood and according to the audience. But the same is true in real life: if instead of you someone else were opposite me at this moment, I would be saying something different. In the theatre, I take my character and "put him on," so to speak, and "smoothe him out" like a suit, and often it's an uncomfortable suit! So I stretch it, and rearrange it, and change things from one evening to the next. I remember that at the hundredth performance of Hamlet, in Paris, I was able to say: "Finally, this evening, I didn't dislike anything I said." But how much suffering during the ninety-nine preceeding evenings! I am an irregular actor, however, and I have failed in my true vocation, which is writing. I didn't become a writer because I chose to become an actor. I chose the physical mode—for acting means living physically. That doesn't mean preferring action to thought — that would be a Fascist concept. But the physicality of acts fascinates me. For example: I love animals, but I recognize that compared to Anna Proclemer, I do not love them, for she needs to touch them constantly. I love them, but it is more abstract with me. I love theatre because I need to be in it physically.

Q.   What was the genesis of *Pilate Forever*?

A.   *Pilate Forever* was conceived not as a well-made play but as a vehicle for saying certain things that we had lived through before saying them. The play was created here [at Albertazzi's villa in Colle Romano near Rome] two years ago by a group of friends, all theatre people, who had resolved to stay here for twelve days without even making a telephone call to the outside world. It's really very hard to get twelve people to stay together for twelve days without communicating externally. It's not easy! How can we possibly think the world will change if it is so hard for twelve people to live together? It's very hard. Anyway, we stayed here. What was the reason for this gathering? None. It was an irrational commitment, but its reality was otherwise: that is, I and the others wanted to settle a matter of long standing — the split between the theatre and our own lives. Life is one thing and theatre another. For years we had conducted experiments and research in psycho-drama together, and then all of a sudden we were performing D'Annunzio. It's totally absurd! If it keeps up for long, it means dying. We will become machines of some kind. That's why many of my colleagues say that theatre is one thing and family another. That's blasphemy! So I threw out an idea, calling for discussion of Christ's revolution and its meaning for us today. What does it mean? Who is Christ? Is it Christ of the Gospels or the historic Christ? Are Jesus and Christ one and the same or two different concepts? These are all themes of modern liberal theology,

of Protestant theology, contemporary Dutch theology —
and on this, *Pilate Forever* is built. The group of twelve
rebelled at first, and a real psycho-drama was created: I
was accused and sued for wanting to do them violence.
But I began writing anyway. I imposed the argument.
Toward the end of the text, as the theatrical discourse
ends, I turn to the audience in order to force a choice between the two symbolic characters that have taken on
life: Barabbas, who represents political revolution, and
Jesus, who represents the revolution of the conscience.
Politics or conscience? Inside or out? Both, perhaps?
That's the choice. But like all new attempts that try to
draw from tradition and from the avant-garde something
that is meaningful for today, *Pilate* does not succeed
completely. It was an attempt to combine song, dance,
mimicry, lyric monologue and dialogue all together.
The result was that it was criticized for discrepancies in
style — which it does indeed have. Complete justice
was not done to the script of *Pilate Forever* due to the
lack of a great director. It requires an outstanding personality to hold together and steer all these sorts of
collective wills. They're going to make a film of it,
directed by Valerio Zurlini. I don't know what will
come of it. Something good, I think, but the movies are
something else yet.

Q.   What do you think of Grotowski?

A.   I have seen only *The Constant Prince*—an extraordinary
play with that extraordinary actor-martyr, Ryszard Cie-
slak. This is absolutely the play that has impressed me
most, personally. I saw in it something that I have been
pursuing from the time I began in theatre. It would be
idle to discuss whether Grotowski's theatre will ever
have a widespread audience. What is clear is that he is an
innovator, and that he is searching. Everything he uses,
however (and it is strange that this sort of theatre was
born in an Eastern European country), is very, very
symptomatic. It is probably a strong reaction against
restrictions, and contains political as well as historical
elements. In the center of the action lies the importance
and weight given to the actor, who not only celebrates
the mass by reciting it, but actually *lives* it. This is, I

think, the highest goal one can achieve — a great moment. He is nude and crude, unmantled, free of anything that masks appearances.

Q.   Have any other plays impressed you so deeply?

A.   Luca Ronconi's *Orlando Furioso.* I saw the première at Spoleto. It was not performed in the open, but in the cellar of a church — a desecrated sacristy, if you will. All that tumult, confusion, spinning and turning back and forth, discovering and following one action instead of another—it all gave a sense of freedom and above all a feeling of participation. You just couldn't get out of it. I think this is the fundamental value of the work: it obliges you to participate without using any form of violence. Ronconi has also done an *Orestiad,* which lasts six hours: the entire trilogy in two evenings. Even though it has been performed in Italy, it is now banned, not for reasons of censorship but because the locale of the production couldn't pass inspection. The *Orestiad* has to be staged in immense spaces, which no legitimate theatre provides, so they have forbidden it.

　　　I also enjoyed very much *Paradise Now,* which I saw in London, more because of the faith of the performers than because of the final product. It's really an alchemistic, initiating process: you are in the initiation hall, and you're risking something whether you remain extraneous or whether you participate, because you are obliged to get into that pile of bodies or to stay out. If you stay out, you feel you are someone who is not alive, and to go in you need a good bit of courage. I have seen the Living Theatre twice in Italy. The first time, in Bologna — *Small Pieces.* There were about twenty people in the audience, and another twenty reactionaries who had come to heckle. The second time, the Living brought *Antigone* to Italy, and the theatre was filled with young people. By now, the dialogue had been established. Young people, as a whole, realized that the Living Theatre was communicating closely with them, and was not simply a display of nudism.

Q.   What method do you use to prepare your interpretation of a character?

A.   This may be a dangerous subject, because when we think a certain theatrical presentation requires a particular kind of preparation, the authorities step in and want everything to "proceed in order." Well, I don't believe you can do things in order. I think selection is automatic and that preparation is not a set of forms to be filled in; that is, it's not a question here of understanding a play in Esperanto, for which preparation is required in order to understand Esperanto. No. It's a question of stripping oneself a little more, of going on stage in a different way from which actors have gone on stage up to now, and you have to be willing to take the risk. People have to be *implicated* in the theatre — it's a horrible word, but it expresses the idea well. We always want to be calm, to know what is going on, and so the world is what the authorities want it to be, because we do not revolt. But Theatre is Revolution! It must be revolutionary. Otherwise it is nothing, or it is something other than Theatre; it is a way of passing time.

Q.   Has the Italian government ever interfered with or stopped one of your performances?

A.   The government forbade for many years the performance of Vitaliano Brancati's *The Governess.* He is one of Italy's greatest writers of the last thirty years. He is famous for his novels, which have been translated into many languages, and several dramas, only one of which —*The Governess*— has been banned. (The play deals with Lesbianism. Interviewer's note.) *The Governess* was banned for as long as censorship existed. I performed in it when the Italian theatre was no longer censored. There is, presently, no censorship of the theatre in Italy. Any play that opposes the penal code is censurable, but otherwise the theatre is free from censorship. But I would no go so far as to say that the Italian authorities don't interfere with the stage through the workings of the law. As in everything else, the authorities can intervene in a thousand ways.

Q.   What type of stage do you prefer?

A.   The open-air theatre fascinates me, with its atmospheric and vocal problems. Several years ago, we put on an outdoor performance; sometimes they are really quite effective. I think that if we define communication my way, then any place is suitable for theatre. If we, for example, right here, now begin to invite others to join us and continue to talk, then have a drink, then start some animated conversation, and then if everyone should express himself, already it would be theatre. That is my definition of theatre. So any place is suitable. I would say that a traditional theatre — the eighteenth or nineteenth century building that houses the theatre in Italy — with its stage and velvet curtain, is very beautiful, but it makes communication difficult. It's more difficult to transform it into a bed. People come and sit down, and the curtain goes up at a certain moment. It's certainly much harder, but not necessarily impossible. The research that is being carried out on theatrical space is very important because it reveals discontentment with the traditional stage, and a series of experiments are resulting from it, based on a desire to create a new stage concept. I saw, in Rome, the Bread and Puppet Theatre, which walked through the streets in big hats for a couple of hours before the show. It was wonderful! That's what theatre is!

Q.   What type of training must today's actor have? Is it different from classical training?

A.   Yes, it is different. Different even from actors' training ten years ago. Up until the 1950's, we were still straddling the traditional actor and the "new" actor concepts. I remember rehearsals in those days: the leading lady, the leading man, the gloves, the exchanges with the company manager. Today, as Olivier says, theatre requires good health — above all, very strong health — and the actor is more and more an athlete or at any rate he is more and more a monster from the psycho-physical point of view. The actor may lose two pounds on an evening, but he puts them on again for the next performance. If he doesn't, he'll die!

Q.   Have you anything to say on the financial problems facing the Italian theatre?

A. That's a very sad note you've introduced. Not that I
    have any way of correcting the situation, but, yes, I have
    something to say. Some time ago, Kenneth Tynan,
    critic-consultant for the London National Theatre, came
    to Italy — to Milan — to see Franco Brusati's *November
    Pietà,* directed by Valerio Zurlini, which is an Italian
    play inspired by Kennedy's assassination. Tynan liked
    it, and wanted to philosophize on the theatre with me.
    I told him there was great confusion between commer-
    cial and artistic theatre in Italy. He couldn't understand
    why, and thought it was very simple to distinguish:
    artistic theatre is State-subsidized and commercial theatre
    is not. I asked him who was to decide which was artistic
    and which commercial. He answered: "Very simple: a
    committee of experts." I replied: "You're very naive to
    think that in Italy it is possible to set up a committee of
    experts which will make objective judgments. When you
    set up a committee in Italy, you've set up a mafia."

Q. Will you tell us more about Franco Brusati's *November
    Pietà?*

A. Brusati is a young dramatist and movie director. He has
    written four plays, two of which I have staged: *The
    Fastidious One* and *November Pietà.* The latter is an ex-
    tremely interesting play. We put it on in 1965. We had
    all been deeply impressed by Kennedy's assassination.
    We were rehearsing *Hamlet* when it occurred. Brusati
    happened to be at rehearsals that very day; when we got
    the news, we were all, naturally, thunderstruck. I said
    to Franco: "Why don't you write a play about this? A
    theatrical company is rehearsing *Hamlet* when the news
    of Kennedy's assassination breaks. Then, unthinkingly,
    the actors assume their roles. Which actor should play
    Kennedy? The King in *Hamlet?* Or Hamlet himself? "
    But this play was never written. It's an idea of mine, the
    type of dramaturgy that I love. Brusati took the idea,
    though, as his point of departure for *November Pietà,*
    whose characters are Oswald and Luca, the latter an
    Italian. To give impact to the objective story of Oswald,
    who assassinates Kennedy, he is seen by an Italian boy
    from the provinces, a kind of Fellini *vitellone* but mean-
    er, a failure in life, who really loves this knight in shining

armour and kills him for that very reason. He imposes himself on the idea of a great man. This was Brusati's idea— a difficult one, because of the duality of the protagonist. The public didn't know whether to sympathize with Oswald or with Luca. It was a hard dramaturgical problem, but it was one of the good, noteworthy plays we put on.

Q.   What are your feelings when you perform in Shakespeare plays? In Pirandello plays?

A.   I have experienced Shakespeare as a reader, just like everyone else; but as a man of the theatre, it is superfluous to say what he represents: he is all of nature; the sea for the navigator; a cataclysm. One returns constantly to Shakespeare. I have done *Romeo and Juliet* both on stage and for television. Then *Hamlet*; and *A Midsummer Night's Dream* many times, because it is the most performed Shakespeare play in Italy. It's a kind of gynmasium for young actors; for example, I have played Lysander under three different directors at different times. I had been working on the play, trying to extract something from it, as Edward Bond did from *King Lear*. Edward Bond is, perhaps, the greatest dramatist living today. Then we saw Peter Brook's version, and, after that, we felt that no one else could ever do *A Midsummer Night's Dream* again, after Brook's spectacular version. The greatness of Shakespeare is that he is always open to any kind of violence. We have a saying in the theatre world in Italy: "You can't kill Shakespeare." If you perform him badly, his work is so resilient that something good must necessarily come out of it. I have also played the role of the Fool in *King Lear*.

　　　　I don't like Pirandello too much, except for a few things such as *Henry IV*. I have directed only one Pirandello play: *As You Desire Me*. We took it to the Soviet Union, too. For me, the Russian public is a kind of poetry. It's an exceptional public, which is totally involved emotionally in a play, so sometimes this creates a limitation in the sense that it is not a critical participation on their part. You get the feeling that you are the protagonists at a huge banquet. The spectators throw flowers on to the stage. Simultaneous translation was provided, but we arranged things so well that not everyone used it: we presented summaries and explanations beforehand. For them, theatre is a feast. To find out what theatre really means to them, it would be necessary to study them historically, politically, and socially. I saw the Moscow Ballet, too, and the feeling was the same. Theatres are always jam-packed. The Russian people enjoy themselves theatrically, as though it were a popular feast. We presented two difficult plays in the Soviet Union: Pirandello's *As You Desire Me*, and, for the first time in the history of the Italian theatre in Russia, Alfieri's *Agamemnon,* which is extremely hard because it is in verse — verse that is hard enough even for us! But this allegory on power was very well understood, and I would say that our two plays were successes.

Pirandello is an author that has done everything himself: he has already foreseen the objections to his work, he has created his voices from the audience, because, poor fellow, the public in his time was even worse than today's. At that time, no one dared interrupt from the floor, so he had to invent the interruptions. In London, I saw Osborne's *Luther,* in which a German indulgence-vendor comes on stage covered with banners and indulgences, turns to the audience and says: "Here are the indulgences of the Holy See and the Pope; whatever sins you have committed — and not only— whatever sins you would like to commit, that you will commit, all will be pardoned as long as you pay." At this point, I heard people in the audience objecting. I asked my friend, Ronald Duncan, an English poet and author, whether the objections had been prepared. He swore that they hadn't. It was really marvelous! Pirandello, to have achieved a similar reaction, would have given up his life — or, perhaps, *Six Characters in Search of an Author*!

To return to Pirandello, we cannot deny his importance with respect to the modern theatre, which originates with him. He was the author who conceived the idea that the character on the stage is his own critic; that is, he is not on stage simply to deceive and mystify the public, but he mystifies himself, too. This is an extraordinary, ingenious idea, which gave rise to the modern theatre. So Pirandello's importance is undeniable, from that point of view. It's rather as an actor that I

don't like him. I'm not interested in playing in Pirandello's dramas. The dialogues are closed; you can't change a
thing. And if I don't change something, I don't enjoy
myself!

Q.   Theatrically speaking, what differences do you discern
between Northern and Southern Italy?

A.   In this respect, Italy is quite an unusual country. I don't
know any other country that is as decentralized as Italy.
In France, what goes on in Paris and in four or five other
cities, in Italy goes on in fifty cities. And since, here in
Italy, fifteen to twenty of these cities have over a million
inhabitants, practically speaking a centralized theatre is
not conceivable, as it is in France or even in America. On
a theatrical tour, you come into contact with fundamen-
tally different audiences. Then there is the language
question: dialects have enormous influence in Italy.
They are part of our authentic, autochtonous culture. So
it happens that the Italian language theatrically does not
exist. It does not exist because the Italian theatre lost
pace during the twenty years of Fascism — very significant years with relation to the European theatre. Fascism nationalized the theatre, and with it a kind of
language — the bad language of the bad translators of
foreign works. So the Italian spoken in the theatre was a
false Italian of false translators, and a false literary
Italian because it was the language of a second literature.
This is important, because after 1945—towards the early
1950's —an attempt was made to revitalize translations of
foreign plays. The Italian authors (with some obvious exceptions) were the same old translators who used a completely conventional language. If you read the texts of
minor Italian authors up to the 1950's, they are startling,
because they read like a parody. A parody of our language. So there is an important basic linguistic consideration. What does language mean in the theatre? Does it
mean simply that the spoken language does not exist in
the theatre? Not really. Because not necessarily does the
theatre have to use everyday language; it does use that
language, too, but it uses language which is a synthesis of
everyday language and literary language. Not even
Shakespeare used a completely spoken language; his

language is poetry. Now there is something else, too. The semantic patrimony of a Neapolitan is not the same as that of a Milanese. So we find, especially in the comic theatre which requires immediate reactions, that much more time is required for the audience to make mental translations. Sometimes we have the impression that we are performing in front of foreigners, because they have to translate into their own terms before reacting. This is extremely important, because it implies difficulties for us in the theatre. Theoretically the same things should not be performed both in the North and in the South. One of the functions of the Stabile Theatres should be just that: the perfecting of a repertory that derives from *local* cultural values. What is the difference between the two publics — North and South? Here I have made a discovery that others, perhaps, have also made. The further South you go, the more conditioned the public is. They say that Northerners are cold, from what it appears. But it's just the contrary. In London, audiences go wild — and they do in Milan and Florence, too. But in the South, it's different. In the South, there is always a defensive silence. Then, afterwards, they let themselves go, naturally. I don't think that this defensive posture depends exclusively on linguistic considerations, but also on the *way* the Southerners have of going to the theatre — that is, their theatrical customs. For example, at the theatre one can express one's feelings freely and not hold them in, but it is clear that since the South has traditions of secrecy, and the Southern woman is supposed to speak little, it happens that on the level of the theatrical public, which is certainly an elite, these traditions continue to prevail, and the Southern lady in the audience, who is really enjoying herself immensely, hasn't the courage to laugh, or laughs with restraint.

The repertory in the South is the same as that in the North because it's supposed to be a traditional repertory. But it isn't. There is a Stabile Theatre in Catania that has tried to build up a repertory with local actors. The have performed Pirandello, Verga, and other authors of Sicilian origin, but they have also produced non-Sicilian plays, which are taken to the North, just as Northern repertories are taken Southwards. The Stabile of Catania did Ionesco's *The Rhinoceros.* To sum up: I

don't think Southern audiences are less evolved than
Northern ones. In fact, I would say just the opposite.
Their behavior is different: they are less extroverted. I
think, though, that the North is more conditioned to
consumer-theatre than the South. The Southerner is
more reflective and more philosophical. All great Italian
thinkers and philosophers are from the South.

The ideal public are the Florentines. The fundamental fact about Florence is its mid-location and its
possession of the language more than any other city. It
was very interesting for me to discover that at my first
performance of Hamlet in Florence, the audience laughed
just when I wanted it to, and in the same places that
London audiences laughed. One can establish a very interesting parallel between Florence and London. There
are cultural reasons for their affinity: the influx of English culture to Florence, inhabited by Englishmen for at
least a century, and a certain intellectual exchange that
accordingly developed between the British and Florentine
intelligentsia. There is no other explanation for their
affinities. When I played the scene between Hamlet and
the King, after Polonius' death, I adopted a very strong
tone of derision and clownish buffoonery, with the
specific intention of amusing the spectators — that is,
Hamlet is in such despair that he derides everyone. So he
amuses himself by provoking the King as far as he can,
inasmuch as he has no more fear of dying or of anything. Generally speaking, the Italian public did not
laugh, thinking that one just doesn't laugh at Hamlet.
It's too serious a play. But they laughed in Florence —
and in London!

Certainly, there are times when we go to regions
of Italy where they have their own language (Sicily, Sardegna, Apulia, etc.) and we wonder whether our audiences will understand us. But they always do.

Q.   Is dialect theatre disappearing?

A.   Dialect theatre is not disappearing, but it is not flourishing everywhere. Sardinian dialect theatre, for example,
does not exist. The great traditional dialect theatres are
the Sicilian, the Neapolitan — Eduardo De Filippo's
above all — and the Venetian. Then there are Genovese

theatrical traditions, which are somewhat marginal, and which are associated with actors like Gilberto Govi when he was alive, etc. The other regions do not have a deeply traditional dialect theatre. The Florentine theatre is a vernacular theatre that comes to life particularly during the summer when the regular theatre is closed. It puts on comedies in the vernacular that have the audiences rolling on the floor. The plays are take-offs on things that are happening in the world. It's a sort of cabaret-theatre on a popular level. As for the Roman dialect theatre, I think its importance is very relative. It seems to me that it's all a question of dramaturgy. In writing, the main thing is to free oneself more and more from correct Italian. We're going in that direction, but more needs to be done. The public isn't ready yet: it objects to theatre that is not in correct Italian, and quickly labels it second-class.

Q.   What are your impressions of the contemporary theatrical scene? Which foreign authors do you most appreciate?

A.   The theatre is suffering a growth-crisis throughout the world today. It remains one of the few vehicles for transmitting culture, and is less conditioned, in my opinion, than literature, music and painting. It is, therefore, a meaningful form of art, which resents all the pressures being put on it from the outside in order to render it a machine. The theatre's rebellion against the machine takes the form of nudity, improvisation, plundering and negation of texts, and the affirmation of man — nude man, in continuous movement, in continuous search, perspiring, bloodied, in shocking makeup. In all of this, there is the will to get back to man, to impose man on us — man for what he is, with all his limitations. So, in my opinion, theatre is living an extraordinary moment. It is a moment of revolt. It is a form of rebellion. This whole flourishing of small theatres, off-Broadway in America, off-Rome, in basements and cellars, is all an attempt on the part of the theatre to refuse traditional showplaces and government subsidies, and the established places where theatre becomes the long arm of power and a way of diverting the bourgeoisie that holds power, and it is therefore a way of seeking its own liberation and its own survival. This seems to be quite widespread, at least in the countries I have visited: in Latin America, New York, London, Paris, Yugoslavia — all the countries I know. In Russia, too, even though there it is more dangerous, and political satire has to take refuge in the underground theatre and the cabaret.

So the theatre is in search of new modes. I can't say that the new modes have been found; I would only say that we are in search of new scenic concepts. There have been attempts, which constitute a sort of model: the Living Theatre, Grotowski, Peter Brook. There are authors who have tried, and even written, innovating texts in which the author no longer is God, and which present spaces. This is what we are looking for: new spaces! We don't want to be good any more. We want to live—that's all. It's different. We have something to say. Arrabal comes to mind. It's enough to think of that allegory of *The Architect and the Assyrian Emperor.* A magnificent text! Spectacular! I'd almost like to present it here in Rome. I saw it in London, directed by the young Victor Garcia, who visited me here three days ago. He would like me to do *The Architect* in Rome. We'll see. I'm undecided whether to do the Arrabal or Bond's *Lear.* Bond is another author who has something concrete to say against violence. And he is courageous, because he renounces easy effects, renounces sentimentality, and goes as far as renouncing plot and dramatic tensions in the traditional sense. It seems that he even renounces poetry in order to say the things he wants to say. But he moves along on his own course. Peter Handke, in Germany, to mention one that I know, is definitely an initiator, even though what he has to say is very difficult and not always accessible. There are other groups and directors, all making similar attempts.

Q.   What can be done in Italy for a true revival of the theatre?

A.   For the moment, one could change certain structures within which the theatre lives today. On the surface, it seems that the existence of the theatre is a settled matter, but it isn't. Absolutely not. This relationship be-

tween the State and the Theatre is a mistake. It is pro-
tectionist, paternalistic, and, worse, it is like giving a
good child a prize. The theatre cannot live within these
constrictions. You cannot force an art, which is constantly moving and dynamic, into bureaucratic conditions
such as we have in Italy. Besides, it's a Bourbon Bureaucracy; it's as though we were all State employees. The
theatre has to be a greater risk than this. If the State
wants to help, it has many ways of doing so. For example, it could start by exempting the theatre from
taxes. Some time back, Franco Zeffirelli and I had the
idea of making an organic proposal along these lines but
we never carried it through, as so often happens. In any
case, exemption from taxes could be a way of giving the
theatre a start. We need a better assignment of space and
facilities to the Stabile Theatres — that is, the theatres
that are completely subsidized by the State; and we need
an exercising of more discrimination from the point of
view of State intervention in the Stabile Theatre, the free
theatre, and the commercial theatre. All of this is missing. Too often, the State's money is used to keep everyone quiet and obedient: handouts here and there.

Q.   The presence of the State, then, accounts for the absence
      of political satire?

A.   Certainly! In part, yes. But I think the absence of
      political satire has still deeper roots than the presence of
      the State. We don't have political satire in Italy because
      the Italian concept of politics is wrong. The political
      figure in Italy is an authority — untouchable! In Italy,
      the carabinier is a god. He is not a man at the service of
      the collectivity; he cannot err. Last year, I wanted to
      produce Brancati's satirical *The Unwilling Don Juan*:
      another forbidden text. (Under Fascism, there would
      have been no question but that it would be banned.)
      It is full of inner violence, aimed against the authority
      of the State (a carabinier), who turnes out to be a homo-
      sexual. They stopped me from producing it. My idea
      was to present a naked carabinier, wearing only epau-
      lettes, sword and boots. Marvelous! This untouchable
      authority who is, after all, a homosexual.
          You have noticed that political figures never

smile. By becoming political figures, they earn privileges
— not duties, but privileges. For them, the family is the
group they belong to. They are not, generally speaking,
humanists. An important subject for discussion in our
times is the relationship between politics and culture.
There is a terrible divergence between the two. Do you
think a Watergate could be possible if politicians were
cultured men? It couldn't possibly happen! Why do
Watergates occur? For this reason: because culture no
longer is in power. It has no influence whatsoever on
power. It is not even engaged in a dialogue with power.
Culture should not be power, but it should have a dialogue with power. In Italy, at the end of 1945, there was
that extraordinary moment of real hope for democracy,
civilian progress and social emancipation. It was indeed
an extraordinary moment for Italy. A euphoria of freedom, after the years of Fascism, gripped the nation.
Theatres were full, and attempts were made to create new
things, but this was all quickly snuffed out by the authorities. Literature was alive; Vittorini founded the review,
Il Politecnico, which is a work of enormous importance,
like *La Nouvelle Revue Française*. But the result was that
Vittorini was thrown out of politics. Togliatti himself
told him to keep quiet and to keep out, because he was
of no use. This is the mistake that the Communists and
the Italian Left made: they should have brought culture
into politics, because culture is always leftist. Today
they are paying for that mistake, and they'll keep on
paying for it. They made the mistake of rejecting culture. The Fascists certainly don't want culture; they
don't want men to think. It's enough to sweat, be strong,
and fight. But the Left had the obligation and the possibility of accepting culture. Yes, of course! I have already cited the example of Vittorini, and there are
others. *Il Politecnico* was worth much more than the
electoral assemblies and some of the other silly ideas
we have. But it was defeated. And what have we today?
A professional class of uncultured politicians who say:
"Albertazzi, he's interesting. What is he doing?" To cite
a pertinent example; when I took *Pilate Forever* to
Brazil, the authorities banned performances in Rio de
Janeiro and Sao Paolo, stating that the play was an of-
fense to religion. (As you know, in Molière's time, *Tar-*

tuffe was banned because it offended religion.) I quickly
asked the Italian authorities for advice. It was a unique
situation for them, because even though the Living Theatre gets itself banned in Brazil, Italy brings Goldoni and
everything goes along smoothly, no? But the first time
an Italian brings a play that arouses political tension, it
is an important event. We were engaging in a cultural act
with *Pilate,* because we were speaking to an authentic
local culture. We were not behaving as Europeans who
perform Goldoni in front of people who are offering their
life's blood for their liberation. How could you expect
them to care about Goldoni? We were bringing culture
into politics, so *Pilate* had authenticity. Well, the answer
that reached me from the Italian authorities was this:
"If you don't perform according to the contract, you
won't receive your subsidy." This was the official reply
from Italy. So I was in danger of having to pay for the
entire tour—about fifty million lire (about $80,000) —
out of my own pocket. The authorities are incredible.
We were scheduled to go to Uruguay, just at the time
people were being killed in the streets. The French
Embassy in Buenos Aires, where the Planchon company
was performing *Tartuffe,* at least assumed the responsibility of telling Planchon not to go to Montevideo. They
advised him to skip Uruguay and go directly to Brazil.
I, on the other hand, had to request an appointment with
the Italian Ambassador in Sao Paolo, who was far from
sending for me on his own initiative. I asked him what
we should do, since the French had decided not to go to
Montevideo. I wanted the Ambassador to share the responsibility for the decision, which was political in part,
since we were taking thirty people into a city where
shooting was going on. But, you see...Pilate! Pilate!
I made my own decision to go to Uruguay. I was glad of
it. I would have gone in any case. But the authorities
shared the responsiblity in no way. Official silence
reigned.

Once there was a round-table discussion in Paris,
with Latin American writers participating — Jorge Cortà-
zar, one of Latin America's greatest living writers, Jorge
Luis Borges, and Ernesto Sabato. The subject of the
round-table was precisely "Politics and Culture". It's
amazing, as well as dangerous, that we do not face the

concept as we should. When politics is only slightly concerned with culture, it is concerned only to the extent
that it forces culture to be subservient to power, and no
more. It does not allow art its imponderable, its demon,
which culture must have. Culture has to be a risk. You
cannot expect culture to propagandize. No! Since power
fears this, it keeps culture out. It knows that authentic
culture, which is, after all, true and authentic politics,
must be free. I am speaking now as a man who is not
politicized in the party sense. The authorities fear culture, and render it marginal, just as the colonial powers
did in Africa: the Italians in Somalia did not permit
black students to go beyond the fifth grade, because
after the fifth grade they became dangerous. Everything is fine up to the fifth grade, but then they mustn't
study any more. Imagine!

Do you know what Senora Marina Brunduarte, in
charge of Rio de Janeiro's censorship bureau, said? The
central authorities had given her the assignment of cen-
soring my *Pilate Forever* — that is, Brasilia had washed
its hands of the matter, not wanting to take any responsibility. They are all Pilates! They decided to pass the
buck to a local censor—Rio de Janeiro's—thereby reserv-
ing the possibility of reversing their own position. Politics, in sum. After reading the play, Senora Brunduarte
exclaimed that it was scandalous, but agreed to watch a
performance. Her reaction was marvel that such a script
and a naked woman could be presented in Italy, and her
decision was that it could not be performed in Rio. I
wasn't allowed to communicate with her. My secretary
spoke to her on my behalf. She said we should put on
our other presentation, which was a collage of various
authors, including Dante Alighieri.[1] So that afternoon,
Anna Proclemer and I, in the presence of Senora Brunduarte, in an empty theatre, with *Pilate* scheduled to be
performed in the evening, presented this collage. When
we reached Dante (we were doing the fifth canto),
Senora Brunduarte exclaimed: "Dante! all right, all
right! even though you must admit that Dante was a
subversive!" That evening, I did not allow the collage
to be performed, but I had the public come to the
theatre, and when it was nice and full, I announced that
the show would not go on. Naturally! Otherwise, I

would have been playing their game! They wanted me to announce that two actors had sore throats and that therefore, for technical reasons, the program had been changed and the collage was being offered instead. And that way, nothing would have happened. But at least I let those hundred, those thousands of people of Brazil, who are really engaged in culture, know that I was on their side. As a matter of fact, Associated Press gave the news out to the world immediately. The newspapers supported us.

I met with two leaders of the Brazilian resistance. They are extraordinary individuals — extraordinary just as long as they keep on fighting, because they, too, when they seize power, may very well become Pilates. But for now, they are magnificent. Magnificent and extraordinary. I sent four copies of the *Pilate* script to four addresses they gave me, and they will stage the play in the *maquis.* Can you imagine? The *maquis,* not in the city, but underground, in the jungle where they live. This is absolutely marvelous! Leftist Catholics there are with the Communists and are working together. *Pilate* is important for them. It has become a symbol. This is sufficient reason for having written *Pilate Forever.*

This whole experience is interesting because so often we speak of political theatre, but actually political theatre is very hard to realize— it exists only when the performers risk arrest. Otherwise, it is not political theatre. When things that are shared by all are discussed, that isn't political theatre. Which is to say that in Italy today, the only possible political theatre would be a Fascist theatre (political on the other side of the spectrum, but still political), or a theatre strongly opposed to the power of the Church, for example. Yes! That would be political theatre.

---

1 Entitled *Collage Number 5,* it contains fragments of works by Dante, Shakespeare, d'Annunzio, Cocteau, Camus, etc. Interviewer's note.

LUIGI SQUARZINA

(Director, Stabile Theatre of Genova)

Q.   Can you tell us something about your early days in the theatre? What kind of training did you receive?

A.   I got my degree in State Directing from the Rome Academy of Dramatic Art in 1945. My first experimental production was an adaptation of John Steinbeck's *Of Mice and Men,* in 1944.

Q.   You were in the United States as a Fulbright scholar about ten years ago. What were the results of your time spent there?

A.   I received a Fulbright scholarship in 1951-52 to attend the Yale Drama School. I travelled all throughout the United States, and saw a great deal of theatre. What was of great usefulness to me was Professor Alois Nagler's method of teaching History of Theatre at the Yale Drama School. After returning to Italy, using Nagler's methodology, I supervised the Theatre Section for the comprehensive *Theatre Encyclopedia* for many years.

Q.   Have you staged any American plays in Italy? What is your general reaction to the works of American playwrights?

A.   I really like the American theatre repertory. I am responsible for the first performances in Italy of Miller's *All My Sons,* Kingsley's *Detective Story,* Wouk's *Caine Mutiny,* Gazzo's *A Hatful of Rain,* and MacLeish's *J.B.* I have also staged O'Neill's *The Iceman Cometh* and *A Long Day's Journey Into Night.*

Q.   On the Italian stage today, so many of the works are by foreign, classical and ancient authors: Beckett, Ionesco, Anouilh, Ibsen, Brecht, Shakespeare, Goldoni, Sophocles, Plautus, etc. Why are *contemporary* Italian dramatists so poorly represented?

A.   I can answer for myself, that as a contemporary author, I have had four of my plays staged: *Tre Quarti di luna (Three-Quarter Moon), Romagnola, La sua parte di storia (History Will Remember),* and *Emmeti (M.T.).* The Italian theatre seeks expression either through a close tying-in with stagecraft, or through historico-political analysis. I have written and staged, in this connection, *Cinque giorni al porto (Five Days in Port): 8 Settembre (September 8th),* and *Rosa Luxemburg.*

> [Interviewer's Note: *Rosa Luxemburg* was written by Squarzina and Vico Faggi and staged by Squarzina himself and Adriana Asti in the title role. Of a documentary nature, the play relates the events —political and personal—in the life of the protagonist of the Spartacist revolt against the German Social Democrats. The Polish-born German heroine was killed by the White Guards in 1919, thus becoming a martyr to the Socialist cause.
> When the play opened in Rome, at the Eliseo Theatre, Luigi Squarzina made a preliminary commemorative speech in honor of Luchino Visconti, evoking the latter's debut as a theatre director in 1946, with Jean Cocteau's *Les Parents Terribles,* at the Eliseo.]

Q.   So the contemporary theatre in Italy does have a socio-political function?

A.   Yes.

Q.   And it is this socio-political function ,that is served by your choice of plays such as *Rosa Luxemburg,* and *The Forest* by Ostrovskiy?

A.   *Rosa Luxemburg* is the dramatization of the life of a revolutionary character and of European history from

1890 to 1919, which still has great significance, even today. *The Forest* is not, strictly speaking, a political play. It is rather a study of the conflict between theatre and life.

Q.   Pirandello's works continue to be presented regularly on the Italian stage. Do you think that Pirandellian thought is still "relevant" today?

A.   Pirandello is, in fact, still very popular today and many of his plays continue to be staged. I think he is still very relevant. My production of *Ciascuno a suo modo (Each in His Own Way)* in 1961, with the troupe of the Stabile Theatre of Genova, probably was responsible for the Pirandello revival in Italy. Other works of Pirandello that I have done are: *Ma non è una cosa seria (But It's Not Serious), Questa Sera si recita a soggetto (Tonight We Improvise), Non si sa come (Nobody Knows How),* and *Il fù Mattìa Pascal (The Late Mattìa Pascal).*

Q.   Does the Italian public today prefer a didactical theatre to theatre for sheer *divertissement?*

A.   The Italian public — and especially young people —is very much interested in didactic theatre, especially if ticket prices are kept low.

Q.   Does the Government interfere in any way with what is done in the theatre?

A.   In Italy, preventive censorship of plays was abolished in 1962. After that date, the magistracy sometimes undertook the stopping or blocking of a production. I personally, together with Ivo Chiesa, who directs the Stabile Theatre of Genova with me, was brought to trial in 1966 on account of my play *Emmetì (M.T.)* The accusations were obscenity and contempt of religion. We were subsequently fully absolved.

Q.   Do you think the Italian Government contributes sufficiently to theatrical enterprises, and are funds channeled in the right direction?

A.   No, Government funds are insufficient.

Q.   What are the differences between audiences in the various cities in Italy? What differences are there between the Northern and Southern audiences?

A.   Your question is much too complicated for me to be able to answer except to say that the North has the advantage of the existence of Stabile Theatres and the possibilities for touring. In the South, there is a great need of government investment in the theatre.

Q.   Julian Beck is presently in Italy. What do you think of the Living Theatre?

A.   The Living Theatre has been very influential in the development of the young Italian theatre. I think Beck's work has been of extreme importance. We even invited him to the University of Bologna.

Q.   Do you think that Grotowski's theatrical concepts allow for communication with audiences?

A.   Grotowski's method offers the actor great possibilities, but it requires a small, sophisticated audience. We have to be sure to distinguish between Grotowski's ideas and the dilettante style that has been an outgrowth of them.

Q.   What do you think the theatre of the future will be like?

A.   Very differentiated, and more and more at the service of our "new" public: the working classes, young people, and old, retired people.

Q.   What kind of structure do you prefer for your presentations: open-air theatre? theatre-in-the-round? with or without proscenium?

A.   I have worked in all types of theatres. I am not in favor of a proscenium.

Q.   How do you choose the members of your troupe?

A.   The Stabile Theatre of Genova has formed a Permanent
         Troupe on a three-year, professional contract basis. I
         demand a great deal of physical and athletic preparation
         of my actors, and I try to awaken all their spontaneous
         capacities and abilities.

Q.   What do you think is the ideal relationship between
         writer, director and actor?

A.   The best thing is collective work — creating together.
         An excellent example is Mousckine's Troupe du Théâtre
         du Soleil.

Q.   Will you tell us what you are working on for the next
         theatrical season (1977)?

A.   I haven't made any decisions yet.

Q.   What are your plans for the future?

A.   I think that, besides direct involvement in the theatre,
         I will devote myself to teaching, at the university level.
         For six years, I have been teaching at Bologna University,
         Faculty of Letters and Philosophy, in the field of Musical
         and Dramatic Arts. This year, I am teaching a theoretical
         and practical course in Stage Directing — the first of its
         kind in Italy. I think that part of the revival of the thea-
         tre in Italy will depend on the University. We need In-
         stitutes of theatrical culture. Here in Genova we have the
         Actor's Library-Museum, which is the outstanding one
         in Italy.

DANIELE COSTANTINI

(Director of the Gruppo Teatro Ottavia—
Italy's youngest stage director)

Q.   Will you give us some biographical details concerning
      your theatrical career?

A.   I started my career at the beginning of 1968. I took six
      months of courses at the National Academy of Dramatic
      Art, but then dropped out because it wasn't stimulating
      and I didn't see the necessity of taking all three levels of
      courses. One of my professors at the National Academy
      for a while was Luca Ronconi. I rehearsed for his play,
      Orlando Furioso, but then got sick and had to leave my
      work. After my recovery, together with some other
      young people, we brought our first play to the stage in
      1969: Michel de Ghelderode's *L'Escurial;* then a Piran-
      dello play: *L'uomo dal fiore in bocca (The Man with the
      Flower in His Mouth).* Then there was an interruption,
      during which I worked in the movies, helping the direc-
      tor. I did three or four films. Then I returned to the
      theatre, and formed an experimental group. Our first
      production was *Il Pazzo e la Monaca (The Madman and
      the Nun)* by Stanislaw Witkiewicz in 1972; the second
      was Aleksandr Blok's *Balagancik* in 1973; then *I Tre
      Grassoni (The Three Fat Men)* by Iuri Slesa in 1974; and,
      finally, last year, *L'Armata a Cavallo (Mounted Army)*
      by Isaac Babel. This year, we're doing something new—
      two new plays, in fact: *La Vita dell'Uomo (The Life of
      Man)* by Leonid Andrejev, and a play based on Robbe
      Grillet's *Project pour une révolution à New York (Project
      for a Revolution in New York).*

Q.   Will you tell us something about the training you re-
      ceived at the National Academy of Dramatic Art, which

you characterized as somewhat useless?

A.   It was outmoded. Actors were trained according to very old-fashioned principles. The actors that come out of the National Academy really do not fit into today's realities. They are of an old stamp. We are still training actors according to Italian pre-war concepts: makeup, cape and sword, diction, etc. — things that, objectively speaking, are useless to the actor today. It's like performing surgery today with nineteenth century techniques — completely inadequate.

Q.   How is Stanislawski's work presented at the Academy?

A.   Stanislawski was taught, but in an arbitrary way. What came out of it was the worst side of his work — if there is a worst side to Stanislawski. In other words, Stanislawski's important contribution was never extracted; it remained secondary. A lot of hazy theory was taught — completely inapplicable, completely removed from theatrical daily practice. I felt a lack of connection between words and practical realization. Moreover, the Academy presented an erroneous theatrical view of Stanislawski. It was not only inadequate, it was erroneous. They gave us a very Romantic view of Stanislawski — not very scientific, whereas in reality there was a very scientific side to Stanislawski's work, which was completely left aside in training our actors.

Q.   How would you evaluate your experience in the movies?

A.   I must say it was a very important experience, because in my later theatrical career, I was able to use a lot of what I had learned. I have done some risky things, though. I use movie techniques for my stage plays, i.e. lights, visual images, sound, and above all the structure of the play. It's a structure based on cinematographic technique. And in this sense my experience in the movies has been most useful in the theatre. Then, too, I brought from the movies a theatrical concept of vastness — a wide visual horizon. My plays always have mass movement scenes, as opposed to intimistic theatre — which I learned from the movies. Almost all the films I worked on were historical films. In fact, I helped make a film in Bulgaria, based on *Michael Strogoff* and adapted from the novel by Jules Verne, in which there are Cossacks, horses, hordes — so it was an action film with mass movement, and it served as a direct, personal and practical experience for me. It taught me how to move thousands of people, how to find the way to fit them all in. I brought all of this to the stage — in a limited space, naturally, but keeping the technical structure of the movies.

Q. Your work seems to be oriented toward Eastern Europe. Why?

A. It's a matter both of choice and education. Having left school early — I left high school after the third year— my readings and cultural choices came from outside the school system. At that point in my life, I had not read Pascoli, Leopardi, Manzoni, or Dante Alighieri. I knew absolutely nothing about them. This was due partly to circumstances and partly to a repulsion I felt for the way these authors are taught in schools. So my exposure to culture depended on circumstances and necessity. It was really chance encounter. For example, the first book that fell into my hands was a collection of poetry by Aleksandr Blok. The book really impressed me. I was fascinated by his poems, by the author, by the period. So that's what I began studying. And that was my education. I began studying Russian history; Russian literary currents, Russian theatre, and consequently these came to form my cultural background. When I devoted myself to the theatre, the plays I chose were drawn from that culture. It's the choice that followed the casual encounter. But the choice is no longer casual when it becomes the real projection of one's own interests.

Q. Having rejected early in your life the traditional Italian classical education, would you say that a classical background is not necessary — or even useless — for someone who has had your success in doing new things in the theatre?

A.   The fact that I have not received an Italian classical edu-
       cation is something I didn't rationalize at the time I
       was living through it. After my success, I realized, on
       the daily, existential level, not on the conscious level,
       that classical education didn't interest me, didn't stimu-
       late me. Culturally, it was much more interesting for me
       to grasp the techniques of contemporary life: understand
       what a video-tape is, for example. Technical education,
       not only in the theatrical field but even in the literary
       field, has had a preponderant influence on me. A book
       or an essay on, for example, the linguistic and structural
       analysis of a novel has always fascinated me more then
       the reading of the novel itself. I have always been more
       interested in studying phonetic changes of the language,
       let's say, than reading the great Italian critic, De Sanctis.
       So these were my choices — which I lived through and
       made out of necessity. Later on I realized that these
       choices suited me best for the things I wanted to do in
       life. I could never have been oriented toward classical
       studies: Torquato Tasso, Dante Alighieri. Of course,
       I've read them, I know them, and, in fact, if anyone asks
       me, I can tell you in what year Dante was born. I will
       even admit that an historical analysis of Italian literature
       should be made and is necessary for someone in the field,
       but it's not a determining factor in my career. I per-
       sonally have learned much more from reading Vance
       Packard than twelve thousand essays on literature. Pack-
       ard's book on the problems of communication, *A Nation
       of Strangers,* has given me the possibility of understand-
       ing the modern world, the directions and limits of to-
       day's society, where we are headed, and how we should
       live.

Q.   So you have been less encumbered by the fact that you
       do not have a classical background, and have been able
       more easily to devote yourself to new theatrical ventures?

A.   Yes. As a consequence of the ideas to which I was ex-
       posed, I was able to develop a new concept of theatre.
       Naturally, not everything is new. I realize that the inno-
       vations that interest me were already foreseen by the
       avant-garde of the beginning of the century — by the
       Surrealists, the Russian Futurists, the Symbolists. But

here, too, I have made a choice. The Russian period 1905-1930 interested me a great deal. It was the period of the birth of the avant-garde, when Meyerhold broke away from Chekhov, to arrive at Blok, and through Blok, Mayakovsky. This was a period of great and total innovation in the theatre from the point of view of technique, structure, recitation, etc.

Q. Apart from Vance Packard, have there been other American influences on you?

A. Yes. Simultaneous with my Russian discoveries, and especially Blok, whom I frequented most from the literary point of view, I made an important discovery: James Baldwin and Le Roy Jones. Their texts influenced me a great deal. I liked their world and their America tremendously. Then, of course, I've read a lot of other Americans. A very useful and interesting book was Charles Wright Mills' *White Collar: the American Middle Class*. The heirs of the "beat" generation, on the other hand, did not have the slightest influence on me — Jerry Rubin, Tom Hayden. I find them unbearable, meaningless.

Q. If you were to put on an American play, which one do you think you would choose?

A. Probably a Le Roy Jones text, *Slave Ship*. Then, what I would love to bring to the stage — but the realities of Italian theatre would make this an extremely difficult and complex project — would be a translation into theatrical images of James Baldwin's novel, *Another Country*.

Q. Russian theatre does not seem to be very well known in Italy. Do the Italians show great interest in what you are doing?

A. What interest they show is real. Just putting on these plays, touring with them throughout Italy, indicates that there is a certain amount of interest. However, as in everything else, Italians are interested and not interested. Interest in the usual sense of the word implies success. Outstanding successes easily become "the style," and people flock to them. My plays, from this point of view, are not "the style," are not successes, and are not highly marketable cultural and theatrical products. So they don't arouse much interest in this sense. Their interest lies in the real force which these plays have. The real cultural force contained in the plays is what makes them interesting.

Q.   Do you think that the theatre in Italy has a socio-political function?

A.   Theatre is part of reality, just as culture in general, culture in the form of economy, politics, etc. are part of reality. Theatre is a moment of reality, from which there is no escape, especially in modern society. Theatre is necessary for the cultural, social, and political life of a country. Concerning the real function of theatre with respect to other forms of expression, I would never say that theatre is more valid than cinema, painting, etc. There is no comparison that can be made. Theatre is theatre; cinema is cinema. There was a point when, for example, with the concept of "poor theatre" first theorized by the Polish director, Grotowski, people spoke about a "poor theatre" as opposed to the great industrial plant that supports the movies. Grotowski says the theatre must not try to substitute for the movies. It must not accept the competition of the movies on the same level. Since cinema has extensive means at its disposal, theatre must not strive for extensive means, but must strive for just the opposite — i.e. "poor theatre," reducing to its bare minimun the theatrical fact itself. Grotowski asks: is the use of light necessary in the theatre? He answers: no, you can do without it. Is music necessary? No, you can do without it. Is a large stage set necessary? No, you can do without it. Then what is necessary? The actor. And what else? The public. Thus, actor and public; a three-two relationship; and from this was born the entire structure and the entire theoretization of "poor theatre." In spite of the attractiveness of an analysis of this sort, in my opinion, theatre that reduces itself to the lowest common denominator of real relationship between actor and public for me means to put theatre on the defensive as compared with movies or other forms of expression.

What I mean is that theatre cannot be the same as other forms of expression, such as movies. So theatre tries to be something that the movies cannot be.

Q. I think it was Jérôme Savary who said that communication is lacking in Grotowski's theatre — that he creates a barrier between the performer and the audience.

A. I agree. I, too, think there is no communication at all. It's too complicated and at the same time too easy. Of course, it's enough for two persons to enter into a physical relationship for an almost invisible relationship to unfold. But just as it is possible to have an intense relationship between actor and audience on the psychophysical level, it is also possible that this relationship can become a deep mystification of a simply enunciated fact: I am here; the spectator is there; I am in a state of tension; I can imagine that the spectator is also in a state of tension. I can say that between us there is a tense relationship. I can say it, but there is no way really of verifying it. So this type of experimental theatre today is backward, as far as I'm concerned. It's a worn out experiment. And I don't see any possibilities for developing it further. For me, the problem is not the opposition of theatre to cinema, cinema to art, etc. For me, modern theatre has to adapt itself to all forms of expression. Theatre in a certain sense is the only vehicle that can synthesize other elements of artistic expression. Theatre can be the synthesis of literature, art, cinema, television. All can be synthesized within the structure of a theatrical performance. Television would never be able to synthesize theatrical structure; nor could cinema, nor painting. So, for me, I think just the opposite of Grotowski: theatre *can* compete, but only by assimilating all other types of artistic expression— cinema, painting, music, etc.

Q. Would the theatrical structure of Ronconi's *Orlando Furioso* be an example of such a synthesis?

A. Yes, because Ronconi used the public as actor in a certain sense. By forcing the spectator to live in direct contact with the structure of the play, Ronconi forces the audience to participate, to move around, not stay seated, not have anything to stare at before their eyes. He created total mass movement. This is part of the assimilation attempt. I think we can go even further. Nevertheless, Ronconi's experiment was extraordinary with respect to the times in which it was presented.

Q.   How was it accepted in Italy?

A.   As usual, at first no one said anything. Everyone was more or less skeptical. People asked: what is it? what isn't it? But after witnessing its great success — and I mean success not in the mundane sense, but real success, that is, finding a counterpart in real life — naturally everyone said it was the work of a genius, great, very interesting, etc., etc.

Q.   What do you think of the Living Theatre?

A.   I think it was a great experiment — one of the greatest in twentieth century theatre, after the period of the Russian and French avant-garde. There was Artaud, and then came the Living Theatre, which was a total life, theatre, and political experience. Even though in recent years the group has not been able to keep up with changes in society, this is quite understandable, because they have lived their theatrical experience as a total abnegation, a total risk, a total danger — not as a privilege. They had no financial backing; they had no security; they had no cultural privileges. There is an analogy to be made in Italy: there is the writer who dies peacefully in his bed after having taught for thirty years at the university; and the writer who dies the way Pasolini did. Pasolini, for all his defects, always lived within reality. It's like the difference between Jean Genet and a member of the French Academy.

Q.   What help does the Italian theatre receive from the government?

A.   The government helps those who already have power. It's very simple. Power buys power. Money buys money. What kind of theatre receives help? Theatre that is tied up with the political parties.

Q.   Does the government control or restrict the theatre in
      any way?

A.   I don't think so. Bureaucracy and economics, however,
      hinder the theatre. It's really very hard to put a play on
      today, unless you are connected with a big organization
      like a Stabile Theatre. For someone who doesn't live
      theatre as a sub-political experience, for someone who
      doesn't enter into the political power-play, it's hard,
      because all the responsibilities fall on your shoulders,
      all the risks are yours. In this sense, then, the govern-
      ment does interfere. On the other hand, I would say
      that today you can do anything. You can't "blame the
      system." That's an outmoded slogan. As for censorship
      — what is it? Nothing, in essence: four individuals who
      look at a film. Generally, they are four imbeciles. It's
      all very casual. There is no rigid system in Italy.

Q.   Will you tell us something about your personal technique:
      how you choose your actors, conduct rehearsals, etc.?

A.   My choice of actors is made instinctively. There is no
      examination, no try-out. I don't look at what the actor
      knows how to do and doesn't know how to do. I don't
      "buy" what the actor offers for sale. We have long
      periods of discussion before beginning rehearsals, we
      discuss our ideas about theatre, then gradually we begin
      discussing the play we are going to rehearse. We focus
      on the idea of the play. Those who survive this *tour de
      force* are those who stay on with me. Those who are not
      up to it generally go their way. They disqualify them-
      selves; I don't have to tell them to leave. If they lose
      interest, maybe they are right, but it's obvious that we
      can't work together.

Q.   Do you read the text for a long time before going on to
      rehearsals?

A.   We never read a text sitting down. We don't rehearse
      around a table. We usually find ourselves in a large,
      empty room; we try to achieve maximum spontaneity in

the reading of a text. Just the way I am speaking now, and moving. We begin to move around the room while reading the text. Each of the actors brings himself into the general mechanism of the text. So we have no traditional rehearsals. No one says you have to say it this way or that way. It seems casual, but everything is obedient to its rythm, its precise plan. Then, slowly, the image of the play emerges. At this point, choice—a certain gesture, a certain look, a certain way of speaking, of moving — enters into the picture. But this is much later on. First, an almost disinterested harmony has to be created — i.e. a way of being together in this space, of reading each other's eyes. It's a very empirical method. It's just part of a personal experiment. You can't write about it as a method.

Q.   What is the relationship between director, writer, and actor?

A.   My group has always chosen texts that have been rewritten or reworked in some way. We have never brought to the stage a text just as it was written. I always rework a text, alone or with my colleagues. This year, there are four of us, some of whom are actors, working on an adaptation. So you can't speak of writer as opposed to actor. Naturally, someone who has no talent for writing doesn't write, but can collaborate on another level, through his intuition and his intelligence. This is how we work things out: I get the idea of putting on a certain play; we discuss it at length; and finally the play is made. So there is no rigid relationship; there are no strict assignments. It's teamwork.

Q.   What type of theatre do you prefer: open-air, theatre-in-the-round, traditional stage with proscenium?

A.   I prefer a space — just like this room, but without walls.

Q.   And the audience?

A.   The audience, depending on the type of play, would put their chairs here and there. Naturally, I have worked in traditional theatres, but I prefer a large circular or rectangular space, and it must be empty. Like a big gym, or a garage.

Q.   Does the empty space make you feel closer to the audience?

A.   No, it's just that I see no need for a place to be labelled a "theatre" or some other space not to be called a "theatre." There is no need to say that a big garage is not a theatre just because there are no seats and no usher to tell you "no smoking." Plays can be performed anywhere: in this room, in an apartment, in an attic, in a gallery, anywhere. Naturally, you have to give some consideration to your public, and not send people down into damp, cold cellars. You have to protect your actors, too, against rheumatism!

Q.   What are you rehearsing for next season?

A.   We're working on a play which is a very free adaptation of Alain Robbe-Grillet's novel, *Project for a Revolution in New York.* It will be performed in March, 1976. At this point, we're concentrating on organizational activities: actors, room for rehearsals, and the very important and complicated theatrical aspect of the work, which requires a lot of preparation — the construction of the soundtrack and the lighting. The basic structure of the play will lie in lighting techniques. The lighting will function like scissors in the preparation of a film strip. So a lot of time will be needed for the preparation of electronic controls to govern the light impulses. Then, in early January 1976, we'll start rehearsing with the actors and discussing the play. We're supposed to be ready for March, but if we feel we're not, we'll postpone for a few weeks. We're supposed to put the play on in a theatre in Rome, but we haven't decided which one because we need an exceptionally large space, and we're looking into the possibility of putting it on in an art gallery.

Q.   How did you go about adapting a novel of Robbe-Grillet, exponent of *l'école du regard,* to the stage?

A.   Earlier, I mentioned structure. How is a novel construct-

ed? It's made up of many elements: language, characters, subjective intervention of the narrator, punctuation.
Robbe-Grillet's novels in particular, and precisely because
he is an exponent of the "school of the look" and because of his capacity for observation of those microscopic
details of real life, allow me to transfer his method of
cognitive investigation in constructing a novel to the
theatre, and to use lighting instead of the pen or instead
of the inner eye of the writer. That is, I use the eye of
the light reflector to discover reality, through montage,
which is not the montage of the novel, but the montage
that comes directly from the movies. So there is that
relationship between the two. The realistic aspect of
theatre also interests me very much. Faces, details,
hands, feet interest me. There is one part of the play
which will receive separate treatment: the crowd — that
is, the visual representation of a crowd through anatomi-
cal decomposition. Just as Robbe-Grillet observes all
the minutest details, which might seem insignificant but
in their totality give a picture of reality, of changes in
reality, of new modes of being—all those can be brought
to the stage through lighting, montage and soundtrack.

Q.   After your performance in Rome, will you take the play
       to the provinces?

A.   Yes, we generally tour all of Italy.

Q.   What differences do you find in the audiences of the
       various regions of Italy?

A.   There is an enormous difference between a Northern
       audience and a Southern one. On the surface, the North-
       erner appears to be more informed and qualified to judge.
       That is, he has seen more plays. But for the quality of
       the relationship between play and public, the Southern
       audience is more stimulating. Criticism that comes from
       the South is generally valid and sincere. Criticism from
       the Northern theatrical spectator is generally very vitiat-
       ed, very intellectualized in the wrong sense of the word,
       very snobbish, a sort of psycho-drama for the sake of
       experiencing cultural intoxication.

Q.   Most of the plays on the Italian stage today are ancient, classical or foreign: Plautus, Shakespeare, Goldoni, Ibsen, Pirandello, Beckett, Ionesco, etc. Why is there such a poor showing of contemporary Italian dramatists?

A.   Because there aren't any. What is written today is unperformable.

Q.   Why?

A.   It's hard to answer. Actually, there is a tremendous number of Italian writers. There are perhaps more writers in Italy than in the U.S.A., which has a population four times greater. The question is why quality is lacking in Italian dramatic writers today. There are many reasons. Apart from Pirandello, apart from the small historical experiment of the Italian Futurists and the ideological independent relationship between the Futurists and the Fascists—apart from these, we have no dramaturgical tradition. I am speaking of the nineteenth century up to now. Our greatest writers have never dedicated themselves seriously and totally to the theatre. Pirandello is the exception. And then, I must say that even though Pirandello was a great dramatist, compared to what others have done in the rest of the world, I don't see his importance. I prefer a thousand times over a text by Blok, Mayakovsky—just to stay in the same time period — to one by Pirandello. This is just my personal reaction. I don't know. Then I think there was the influence of Fascism in the 1930's, which impeded cultural and, especially, theatrical development. The dramatist must live in contact with changes in the theatre in a technical and practical sense. He can't stay isolated from the stage and write.

Q.   Would you say that Pirandello's theatricality is inapplicable today?

A.   Pirandello's theatricality is totally irrelevant to today's realities. There is absolutely nothing at all in Pirandello's characters that relate to today's world.

Q.   Have you seen *Artaud at Rodez* that is currently being performed in Trastevere?

A.   No. I don't know anything about Marowitz' experi-
        ments. I know some of the things he has written, but I
        don't share his ideas.

Q.   In your opinion, is the cabaret a form of theatre to be
        considered seriously?

A.   In my opinion, cabaret in Italy today is horrible. It's a
        sub-product, a sub-culture. Naturally, you can't compare
        it with *fin de siècle* cabaret, which was worthwhile. Our
        cabaret in Italy today is nothing but television sketches.
        Horrible.

Q.   Will the theatre survive?

A.   For me, theatre is an irreplaceable means of communica-
        tion.   Laser will change the movies completely. We'll
        reach the point where the screen won't exist anymore.
        We'll be projecting photographic, cinematographic,
        moving images into the air. So cinema will not survive,
        in this sense. Not so for the theatre. Theatre will always
        be. If theatre is my relationship with you, my human,
        physical, material relationship with you, it has no sub-
        stitute. What might be said is that in the future, we may
        no longer need this relationship. Maybe. I don't know.
        Someone who shares my views in this respect is another
        young stage director, my friend Memè Perlini. He is able
        to create an exceptional relationship between himself,
        his actors, and his audiences, transporting all of them into
        his own world of dreams, fantasies, memory, torment and
        imagination. Memè Perlini is now working on a new play
        based on Raymond Roussel's Surrealist prose poem,
        Locus Solus. The play should open soon at the under-
        ground theatre "Attico", in Via Cesare Beccaria. Perlini
        has taken only the basic feelings—loneliness, revolt and
        escape from reality — from the Roussel text, and con-
        verted them into visual and sound images. He uses voices,
        faces and bodies to communicate and to bewitch the
        audiences' senses.
                So I have great faith that theatre will survive, and
        the Roman school of *avant-garde* theatre is helping.

ROBERTO MAZZUCCO

(Playwright)

Q.   Would you give us some biographical details as they relate to your theatrical career?

A.   I was born in 1927. Here are some highlights of my theatrical activity: my principal plays are *Adamo e il buon rimedio (Adam and the Good Remedy)*, first presented in Rome at the Satiri Theatre in 1958; *Uguali e Tanti (Equal and Many)*, first presented in Bologna at La Ribalta in 1963; *I Giovenchi (The Young Oxen)*, first presented in Sicily at the Stabile Theatre of Catania in 1968; and *In nome di Re Giovanni (In the Name of King John)*, first presented in Rome at the Arti Theatre in 1972. In addition, fourteen of my one-act plays have been performed. I'll mention *Tre Italiani (Three Italians)*, which has had several revivals, *Come si dice (As They Say)*, which ran for 250 performances, and *L'inflazione (Inflation)*. The last two have been performed in the United States, at Providence Playhouse and at Hunter College. *Piove sulla libertà (It's Raining on Liberty)*, translated by R. Absalom and published in *Drama & Theatre*, has been performed in the United States. As a matter of fact, one-acters and cabaret are my main theatrical interests. I founded the Ripa Kabarett Theatre in Rome, where I have presented several shows, most notable of which is *Vilipendio e altre ridicole ingiurie (Contempt and Other Ridiculous Insults)*. I have won the following theatrical prizes: Piccolo Teatro di Milano (1954), Alfieri (1956), Swiss Radio (1961), Riccione (1964), and Vallecorsi (1965). The play that won the Vallecorsi prize, *L'andazzo (The Fad)*, has had five radio performances.

         In addition, I have written radio dramas, movie

and television scenarios, and done some translations. With *Aspettando Jo (Waiting for Jo)* by Magnier-Coppel, which I translated and adapted, I participated in the opening of the Dorelli-Spaak theatrical company. I have also written essays on the theatre, some of which have been translated and published abroad (especially *Plays and Players*). An essay on the theatre of Dario Fò has been used in our schools and has been translated into five different languages.

Q.   Why and how did you become interested in the theatre? How would you characterize your first work?

A.   I found the theatre to be a congenial form of expression inasmuch as it finds immediate confirmation in the public's reaction and permits incredible synthesis in a line or a dialogue. The theatrical prizes bestowed on me early in my career led me to continue in the medium, to the detriment of other literary experiences. My first work was *Piove sulla libertà (It's Raining on Liberty)*, written in 1951, in a style that preceded Ionesco. In Italy, however, innovators are not easily accepted, and my text had to wait eleven years before it was performed. Italian theatrical managers prefer proven foreign plays rather than risking something new, something experimental. Also, there is a century-old Italian subjection to foreign culture — especially French — particularly evident in the theatre: it suffices to think of the nineteenth century.

Q.   Are you Roman? Has your regionalism influenced your theatrical work in any way?

A.   I was born in Rome, but of a very heterogeneous family: ancestors from the Abruzzi, Piedmont, etc. So I have no sense of regionalism, but rather of a persistent tension in the face of the nation's problems.

Q.   What do you express above all in your work?

A.   I feel that satire is the dominant characteristic and the most "necessary" one. Satire is the literary form best suited to the Italian spirit and language. All other forms seem to me to be imitations or imports. As far back as antiquity, Horace had defined satire as *italum acetum.* The most "Italian" authors are satirical authors: Giulio Cesare Croce, Ruzante, to Dario Fò in our times. Even the *commedia dell'arte,* despite its servility and lack of ideas, was a satirical phenomenon.

Q.   Are your writings linked to each other through some common denominator?

A.   My writings are generally satirical. One critic has pointed out that even in the diversity of their subjects and characters, there is always the basic condition of rejection — someone who tries to find his place in society but for some reason or other is always excluded.

Q.   Are your characters logical? irrational? symbolic? realistic?

A.   I prefer realism to symbolism. Satire, however, leads us ineluctably to the grotesque and the surrealistic. I am absolutely opposed to irrationalism. Irrationalism is a convenient way for authority to subjugate the masses, but the irrational is simply that which has not yet been scientifically revealed or explained.

Q.   If you were to judge your own work or express your personal opinion on what you have written, what would you say?

A.   I should have been more courageous, more coherent, more implacable. Often the so-called requirements of the stage have functioned as a braking force. Moreover, I recognize in my work a residue of sentimentalism which I have not yet succeeded in eliminating and which I ascribe to my humanistic education and to family vicissitudes.

Q.   In your opinion, does the Italian contemporary theatre serve a socio-political function?

A.   In Italy, as everywhere else, the theatre has a socio-political function. Theatre is a political event.

Q.   Do you think that the Italian Government contributes
       sufficiently and in the right way to a renewal of the
       theatre? What more could be done?

A.   The theatre is sufficiently helped by the Italian state as
       far as subsidies go, but support is given in the wrong way.
       In my opinion, a purely commercial group, motivated
       solely by profit, should not be subsidized. It is inadmis-
       sible for the state to help anyone whose purposes are not
       cultural. Moreover, there are injustices: the Stabile
       theatres, eight in all, recruit about one-fifth of all the
       spectators, they perform about one-fourth of the plays,
       but they rake in about one-half of the state subsidies.
       Finally, the state should not aid anyone who does not
       help promote a national repertory.

Q.   Does the Italian Government interfere in any way in the
       theatre?

A.   Not directly, but by saddling the theatre with excessive
       audits, permits, authorizations, etc. —remnants of the
       past regime— the state ends up by exerting a negative in-
       fluence on free theatrical expression.

Q.   In what direction is contemporary Italian theatre headed?

A.   The Italian theatre is strongly politicized in its basic
       reality, but it avails itself almost exclusively of the
       classical authors you'll find in the repertories of the
       Stabile theatres and the other big companies. An ob-
       jective which seems vital to me is the *regionalization* of
       theatrical structures to permit the emergence of local
       realities.

Q.   To what type of play does the Italian public react with
       most enthusiasm?

A.   The contemporary spectator reacts to any play that lays
       bare the particular social problem that most concerns
       him.

Q.   As you indicated earlier, Italian theatrical managers rely
       on proven works. Indeed, in recent years the billboards

are dominated by Sophocles, Plautus, Shakespeare, Ibsen, Brecht, Pirandello, Ionesco, Beckett, etc. Why are the dramatic works of contemporary Italians not easily received, assuming they are not avant-garde or "innovations"?

A.   There are historic, political and cultural reasons. Italians have always been adapters of texts rather than original creators, beginning with Plautus and Terence, and ending with our numerous contemporaries who Italianize novels and classical texts. The natural tendency toward satire, from the scurrilous ancients to the present burst of cabaret authors, has brough a fragmentary, brief production of short duration. It is not by chance that Italy produces splendid one-acters rather than plays *per se.* (In this quantitatively reduced space of the one-act I recognize myself also.) It is a national characteristic. Our narrative literature is richer in short stories than in novels; in Italy, the *roman-fleuve* is rare and unsuccessful. I think that climate plays a part in this. The long Russian winter is in great part responsible for the long Russian novels.

So the irruption of foreign plays has always found easy entry on to the Italian stage. Then there are political reasons: national authors would naturally treat domestic themes and problems of current social import. Censorship in the past, and the conditioning of today, give rise to a preference on the part of theatrical producers for classical and foreign texts, which are less risky or dangerous.

Cultural reasons: to give space to a national repertory, there is need for great courage — even personal courage —love of risk, and passion for what is new and experimental. But instead, the play that has already been proven abroad is preferred, because our theatrical producers fear a failure. Such fear derives from their academic, scholastic education, far removed from the realities of everyday life, and also from their subjection to the state's financial help, which often is politically discriminatory.

Q.   What is your opinion of Brecht?

A.   An important author who has had a vast influence on
the theatre.

Q.   Has any foreign writer inspired you?   In what way?

A.   I have had many loves; I don't know whether they have
influenced me. I loved Camus for the human dimension
he gave to political problems; Ionesco interested me because he rid me of my fear of the absurd and eliminated
my self-criticism. As far as dialogue goes, I have always
been fascinated by certain Americans: Odets, Irving
Shaw, etc.

Q.   Which authors have played an important role in your
artistic and intellectual evolution?

A.   At first, Shakespeare.   Then the Expressionists and
Crommelynck.   I would ascribe the greatest influence,
however, to narrative writers and essayists, rather than
to playwrights. Pavese above all.

Q.   Which contemporary playwright do you prefer? Which
is your favorite contemporary play, and why?

A.   That's a hard question.   Generally speaking, I always
like Fò, often Pinter, and sometimes Weiss. The best
play of the past decade was Dario Fò's *Mistero Buffo*.

Q.   What do you think of "communal theatre" as interpreted by Garcia, Savary, and the Living Theatre?

A.   Important, but belonging in the vein of ritual theatre,
to which I am not attracted. I prefer the other vein—the
politico-social. I'm happy to note that the Living Theatre, the only great theatrical revolution (because after the
Living, theatre became something else), is abandoning
ritual and drawing closer to politico-social themes.

Q.   What are the functions of a director, in your opinion?
Would you like to direct your own plays? Who are the
directors of your plays?

A.   The director is a co-ordinator, not a co-author. I have no desire to direct my own plays. My principal directors are Ruggero Jacobbi, Carlo D'Angelo and Nino Mangano.

Q. What kind of stage do you prefer for your works? An outdoor theatre, a traditional stage, an amphitheatre, a theatre-in-the-round?

A. Anywhere, as long as the stage sets are minimal. The best stage is the public. Conclusion: theatre in the public square.

Q. Do you go to rehearsals of your plays? What is your relationship with the actors?

A. From time to time I may go to a rehearsal, but generally speaking, rehearsals bore me. My relationship with the actors is excellent from the human point of view. Often I have the impression that I would recite my lines differently from them. Not better, just differently.

Q. Would you mention the names of some actors and actresses who have performed in your plays?

A. The principal ones are: Antonio Pierfederici, Giustino, Durano, Antonio Salines, Magda Mercatali, Silvio Spaccesi, Marisa Belli, Alberto Terrani and Paolo Bonacelli.

Q. Are you writing another play at this time? What are the major difficulties you encounter when writing?

A. I am writing a satirical comedy about the Center-Left, so it's a political play but for the general enjoyment. I like to make corrections more than I like to invent. Inventing is hard work, while polishing is a diversion. The greatest difficulty comes from the nuisances that surround us: lack of peace and quiet, the telephone.

Q. What are your plans for the future?

A. To write.

GASTONE MOSCHIN

(Stage and Screen Actor)

Q.   Where did you receive your early training? Which is the first play in which you performed?

A.   I recieved my early training in the Stabile Theatre of Genoa. The first play in which I performed was *Ivanov* by Chekhov.

Q.   Are you Roman or from another region of Italy? Has your regionalism affected your work and your career in any way?

A.   I am from Verona in the Veneto region, but my regionalism has never affected either my career or my work.

Q.   You recently performed in Orvieto in the Polish play, *The Emigrants,* by Mrozec. What was the Italian reaction to the play?

A.   The Italian reaction to this play is a positive one, but I think that any public would react positively to a good play on the subject of freedom. Freedom is the very aspiration of man. I could go on at length on the subject, but I prefer to be brief, and will say simply that I am very sensitive to the problem of freedom. Most important, I have no great sympathy for so-called intellectuals, and in this I fully share Mrozec's point of view.

Q.   What differences do you perceive in your audiences as you tour the various regions of Italy?

A.   I am now on tour, performing in Mrozec's *The Emigrants.* Do not forget that in Italy there is a great difference between the North and the South, especially from the cultural point of view. Obviously — and it's a pity to have to say it — I prefer performing in the North and Center of Italy rather than in the South.

Q. What is your general impression of contemporary theatre as opposed to classical?

A. A certain type of play is called classical for the simple reason that it's always contemporary, whereas a contemporary play in the real sense of the word most often will not become a classic.

Q. What do you think of Grotowski?

A. I'm ashamed to have to say it, but I can't express any opinion because I don't know Grotowski well enough.

Q. In what kind of theatre do you prefer performing: open-air, theatre-in-the-round, with or without proscenium?

A. I prefer performing in a theatre with a proscenium.

Q. What techniques do you use in preparing a role?

A. In Italy, the techniques of Copeau, Stanislavsky and Brecht — alienation—are used, according to the theatrical work involved.

Q. Which has been your favorite role, either for the cinema or for the stage?

A. My favorite stage role was Piotr in Dostoyevsky's *The Possessed.* I really felt the part deeply, and I'm attached to it sentimentally because it marked my successful debut in the theatre (after *Ivanov*).

Q. Do you see the theatre as having a social or political role in Italy today?

A. Yes, the theatre in Italy today tends to assume a political and social role. Workers, students, and farmer have formed theatrical cooperatives, but, naturally, they receive a favorable reaction from the public only if they really put on a good play. Dario Fò's company is doing very well.

Q. Do you feel that the Government interferes in any way in the Italian theatre?

A. The Government interferes in the Italian theatre, not directly through censorship, but indirectly by subsidizing private companies, cooperatives, and public theatre in different ways and according to the repertories that the companies intend to perform.

Q. To what kind of theatrical production do Italians today react most positively?

A. Generally speaking, Italians accept "boulevard" comedy most easily. Strehler, however, has always been remarkably successful.

Q. In what direction is the Italian theatre headed, in your opinion?

A. I would say that it's headed in all directions.

Q. Has the State given sufficient support to the dramatic arts in Italy? What more could be done?

A. Naturally the theatre could be helped more, but I think that in view of economic conditions in Italy today, as much as possible is being done. In any case, the biggest subsidies go to the opera, and that, too, is understandable.

Q. Would you tell us how you feel about the differences between acting for the screen and for the stage?

A. Thanks to technical means, cinematography puts word and gesture into perfect focus, whereas acting on stage, the actor must rely on his own means and ability.

Q. Do you ever change your interpretation during rehearsals?

A.   No, not the over-all interpretation, although I might change details.

Q.   What are your future plans?

A.   I hope to make a good film during the summer of 1976, and next year I will bring *The Emigrants* to the big cities of Italy: Rome, Milan, Genoa, Florence.

INDEX

THE ITALIAN THEATRE TODAY

Composed in IBM Selectric Composer *Journal Roman* and printed offset by McNaughton & Gunn, Incorporated, Ann Arbor, Michigan. The paper on which the book is printed is The International Paper Company's *Bookmark;* the book was sewn and bound by Howard Dekker & Sons, Grand Rapids, Michigan.

The Italian Theatre Today is a Trenowyth book, the scholarly publishing division of The Whitston Publishing Company.

This edition consists of 550 casebound copies.